Comparative Contract Law

National legal systems have their own principles and rules on contract law. The trans-nationalization of trade and legal practice involves acting in the context of legal diversity.

This book provides an introductory overview of the main issues of contract law from a comparative perspective, focusing on the legal traditions of civil law and common law.

Featuring short theoretical overviews, followed by cases selected from various jurisdictions, the book shows the concrete application of the principles and rules involved.

Civil law and common law represent two different models of dealing with contract law issues. The book focuses on the French, German, and Italian experiences and on the English legal system, the latter being the main source of inspiration for other common law countries, with some significant exceptions. Topics covered include the structure of contract law and the rules about its formation and interpretation, the role of pre-contractual negotiations, the consequences of mistakes, and breach and supervening events (including the impact of the Covid-19 pandemic). Readers will learn about common problems that are faced when contracting with parties coming from different jurisdictions, whilst also acquiring a deeper understanding of the approach of their own legal system.

This book will be key reading for undergraduate and postgraduate students of comparative contract law, and contract law more generally.

Ermanno Calzolaio is Full Professor of Private Comparative Law since 2006. He was Dean of the Department of Law at the University of Macerata, Italy, between 2012 and 2018, and has also been a visiting professor at universities around the world (Australia, China, France). He is also a member of the board of the Italian Association of Comparative Law (AIDC), the International Academy of Comparative Law and the Italian Evaluation Board for research in law.

Comparative Contract Law

An Introduction

Ermanno Calzolaio

Routledge
Taylor & Francis Group
LONDON AND NEW YORK

Cover image: @ Getty Images

First published 2022
by Routledge
4 Park Square, Milton Park, Abingdon, Oxon OX14 4RN

and by Routledge
605 Third Avenue, New York, NY 10158

Routledge is an imprint of the Taylor & Francis Group, an informa business

British Library Cataloguing-in-Publication Data
A catalogue record for this book is available from the British Library

Library of Congress Control Number
2021950625

ISBN: 978-1-032-17056-5 (hbk)
ISBN: 978-1-032-17053-4 (pbk)
ISBN: 978-1-003-25160-6 (ebk)

DOI: 10.4324/9781003251606

Typeset in Optima
by Deanta Global Publishing Services, Chennai, India

To my wife Rosalba

Contents

1 Introduction

1.1 Why study comparative contract law?

Used both in daily life and in economic activities, contract is perhaps the most widespread legal institution. In every legal system, contract law rules are often very complex and they cover a large spectrum of issues, from the beginning of the life of the contract until its end.

In the contemporary world, transactions are frequently entered into on a cross-border basis. Consequently, the trans-nationalization of trade and legal practice involves acting in a context of legal diversity. Contract law principles and regimes differ from one country to another and legal education cannot ignore the need to go beyond one's own legal system when dealing with each legal issue.

The word 'contract' itself has not the same legal meaning everywhere. It would be a mistake to assume that one's own legal system understanding is necessarily the same as another one. For instance, English law has no formal definition of contract and has not needed one,[1] whereas all the continental legal systems (France, Germany, Italy, etc.) define contract in their civil codes. Moreover, even when definitions do exist and they seem similar, one should be aware that reality could be very different from appearance. A simple example can illustrate this point. Imagine that an Italian student meets a Chinese colleague and asks him about the definition of contract in China. His answer will be simple, quoting Article 464 of the new Chinese Civil Code approved on 28 May 2020 and in force from 1 January 2021: "A contract

1 E. McKendrick, *Contract Law. Text, Cases and Materials*, 9th ed., Oxford University Press, Oxford, 2020, p. 3.

DOI: 10.4324/9781003251606-1

refers to an agreement between the parties to civil legal relations for the establishment, modification, termination of a civil legal relation".[2] The Italian student will immediately think of the Italian Civil Code definition, according to which "a contract is an agreement between two or more parties in order to establish, regulate or terminate a patrimonial legal relationship" (Article 1321). The similarity is evident and the two students could conclude that their legal systems share a common understanding of contract. Such a conclusion would be inaccurate and misleading.

It is intuitive to realize that a disagreement about 'what' a contract is can create obstacles while entering into cross-border transactions. Hence, it is unavoidable for a jurist of the 21st century to adopt a comparative approach in order to broaden the sometimes too narrow national horizons of legal studies and to unveil where differences and similarities lie.

1.2 The comparative approach

What does 'comparative approach' mean? This is not the place to focus on the much-debated issue concerning the aims and methods of comparative law, which has always attracted the attention of comparatists, engaged in giving reasons concerning the utility of their field of study. Neither is it possible to show the contribution of history, too often neglected, which shows to what extent a comparative approach to the legal phenomenon is inherent in the development of the Western legal culture.

More simply, the following remarks aim at reminding readers that comparative law is a 'strange' subject in legal studies.[3] It is a way of looking at legal problems, legal institutions and entire legal systems based on the acknowledgment that the legal phenomenon is universal and relative at the same time. It is universal because every community of human beings implies at least a minimum level of normativity. It is relative, because the ways in which each community conceives and applies its rules can vary, even substantially,

2 Art. 464 of the Chinese Civil Code reflects the definition adopted by the Contract Law PRC 1999 ("a contract means an agreement on the establishment, alteration or termination of a civil right-obligation relationship between natural persons, legal persons or other organizations as subjects with equal status").

3 As pointed out in the well-known textbook *Schlesinger's Comparative Law*, 7th ed., New York Foundation Press, New York, 2009, p. 2.

according to the different social, historical, political, religious and economic contexts.

In this sense, comparative law is a cognitive process having a circular movement. It goes from one legal system to another and from the latter it comes back to the former, enriching the knowledge of the specific features of each of them, together with the aspects they have in common. The study of one specific foreign law, seen as 'other' in relation to one's 'own' law, leads not only to the knowledge of the foreign law under scrutiny, but it also has an added value, designated as the 'reflective quality of comparison'.[4] It means that through the comparative method "it becomes possible to make observations and gain insights which would be denied to one whose study is limited to the law of a single country".[5] Recalling the incisive words of the outstanding Italian comparatist Gino Gorla, "an 'individual' does not exist without the 'other'".[6]

In the 20th century, the distinguished French comparatist René David stated that it is "superficial and false" to conceive law simply as a set of norms in force in a given country. He noticed that each legal system uses a specific vocabulary, it regroups its rules in specific categories and is connected with a particular conception of the social order. 'Difference' in law has to do with all this and therefore it is not to be reduced to the variety of legal rules in force in a specific territorial ambit.[7]

Accordingly, the theory of legal systems (or legal traditions) was shaped in response to the need to study law as a phenomenon that varies in time and in space. It aimed at setting criteria in order to define the identity of a legal system or of a group of legal systems (a legal style), in relation to some durable elements that characterize a specific legal experience, beyond the differences existing in the various national legal orders.

Many classifications have been suggested, but each one is relative and approximate, so it has to be taken cautiously, as it only has a descriptive value. However, with this note of caution in mind, one should not underestimate the merits of the theory of legal systems. It played a decisive role against the self-referentiality of the legal discourse, accentuated by the trend

4 L. Moccia, *Comparazione giuridica e Diritto europeo*, Giuffrè, Milan, 2005, p. 95 ff.
5 Schlesinger, p. 2, ibid.
6 G. Gorla, 'Diritto comparato' in *Enciclopedia del Diritto*, vol. XII, Giuffrè, Milan, 1963, p. 928.
7 See R. David, *I grandi sistemi giuridici contemporanei* (R. Sacco ed.), CEDAM, Padua, 2004, p. 16.

of legal positivism and its dogmas, with the result of enclosing the role of jurists in a sterile exercise of analysis and application of legal rules enacted by the legislature of each country. The consequences of this approach have not completely disappeared and still now, especially in the civil law countries, it is often taken for granted that law is to be identified by the rules enacted by the legislature.

1.3 The common law/civil law distinction

Among the various legal traditions (or 'families'), within the 'Western' world comparative law scholars traditionally distinguish (and often oppose) civil law and common law. Civil law embraces all the legal systems sharing the Roman law heritage and having adopted civil codes (France, Germany, Italy, Spain, Latin-American countries, etc.). Common law refers to the English legal tradition, having influenced many legal systems, such as the United States, Australia, Canada, New Zealand, etc., being not codified.

The differences between the two legal traditions are commonly summarized as follows. First, the legal mentality tends to be more deductive in the civil law countries and more inductive in the common law ones. Second, in the civil law countries statute law continues to be the 'sole' source of law, in contrast with the common law world where case law is a source of law alongside statute law. Third, judicial styles differ consistently, to the point that nothing comparable to the attention to the facts given by common law judges in their decisions can be found in any civil law country.

The civil law/common law distinction is questioned nowadays. Their differences are often over-emphasized. Moreover, they are seen as representative of a geographical dimension of the legal phenomenon that does not fit anymore with the contemporary world. It is no longer possible to consider civil law and common law in terms of a geographic dichotomy, because not only are both traditions outstanding expressions of a common history of European law[8] but also because their study leads to the discovery that some specific attitudes that characterized each of them in terms of separation have now become integrated. Just to give an example, the relationship between statutory law and case law is changing both in the civil law tradition (where

8 G. Gorla, L. Moccia, 'A "Revisiting" of the Comparison between "Continental Law" and "English Law" (16th–19th Century)', *The Journal of Legal History* 1981, 2(2), p. 143.

judges are no longer, if they ever were, the 'mouth of the law', as assumed the French jurist Montesquieu) and in the common law tradition (where legislation is growing and reaching almost every field of law).

However, echoing again René David's words, it would be "superficial and false" to draw the conclusion that no difference exists at all between the civil law and the common law systems. In particular, some argue that they are converging because in the common law countries judges are increasingly urged to interpret and apply statutes, whereas their civil law colleagues are enlarging their field of action as a consequence of the increase in legislation. This conclusion is clearly contradictory. From the same phenomenon (increase of legislation), it draws two opposite results: the bureaucratization of the role of judges in the common law systems and a more creative role in the civil law ones. The truth is that in both legal traditions one can find evidence of new ways to conceive the role of judges and shape the techniques of judicial interpretation and legal reasoning.

Without entering into further details, the distinction between civil law and common law continues to be relevant, at least in the field of contract law. Both legal traditions move from the idea that a contract arises if the parties want to be bound, but the role attributed to the parties' will is different, sometimes with significant outcomes. For this reason, we will assume the distinction for didactic purposes being emblematic of two different attitudes that somehow co-exist in both legal traditions.

Another preliminary methodological point needs to be clarified. Nowadays, it is more and more difficult to consider the civil law and common law traditions as a whole. Within the civil law systems, the rules on contract law often differ substantially and thus elude a unitary consideration. We will concentrate our attention mainly on the French, German and Italian experiences, being the most influential also in other countries. In a specular way, within the common law world, English law of contract was the model to which Australia, Canada, New Zealand, Singapore and the United States were heavily indebted until the first half of last century. Now, these legal systems have gradually adopted original and specific solutions.[9] In particular, in the United States, despite the fact that private law is not a federal matter (being within the competence of each state) the rules tend to be quite homogeneous and

9 E. Descheemaeker, 'Comparative Common Law', *Revue Intern. Droit Comparé* 2020, 4, p. 915 ff.

they sometimes differ markedly from their English origins. For this reason, even if we will mainly consider English contract law, it being the common source of inspiration of the common law way of reasoning, we will also try to highlight the main differences in respect of other common law countries.

1.4 Aims

The idea behind this book arises from a pedagogical need. Literature on comparative contract law is impressive. One could easily desist from setting out on a risky adventure as approaching such a wide field of study. However, textbooks and treatises on comparative contract law are either very long (not suitable for an academic course) or they focus on theoretical issues, which are indeed extremely important, but not appropriate for a preliminary approach.[10]

This book does not cover the various contract law regimes in the entire world. Studying comparative contract law is unavoidable, as we previously observed. However, it would be impossible to embrace all the legal systems. Nevertheless, a short introduction can be useful to suggest a method to face the different conceptions, together with providing basic information about the most relevant topics. Our wish is to introduce the reader (students and legal practitioners interested in the international dimension of legal trade) to the various dimensions of contract law, in order to acquire the relevant keys to understanding.

1.5 Judicial styles

Short theoretical presentations of the main principles and rules will introduce the study of cases of different jurisdictions addressing similar problems. Considering the various doctrines in their practical application will allow grasping similarities and differences going beyond a theoretical approach.

In this respect, the reader will realize that judicial styles differ consistently.

Under the expression 'style of judgments', comparatists attract attention to the importance of considering the different styles that judges adopt while

10 Cf. T. Kadner Graziano, *Comparative Contract Law. Cases, Materials and Exercises*, 2nd ed., Elgar Publishing, Cheltenham, 2019, p. 5 ff.

drafting their decisions, in particular the language used (concise or detailed), the structure, the ways of presenting the facts and the legal issues involved, the reference (or the absence of any reference) to previous decisions, the recourse to academic writing in order to support the decision and the presence of separate (either dissenting or concurring) opinions. All these aspects are sometimes neglected, but they are extremely important, as they reveal the relations between statute law and case law and the conception of law followed in a given legal experience.

Moreover, a reader coming from the common law tradition should not be misguided by the fact that separate opinions are usually not admitted in civil law. The decisions adopted by the Supreme Courts are collegial, i.e. judges vote secretly, and if one of them disagrees with the conclusion reached by the majority, this will not be indicated, nor will a separate (concurring or dissenting) opinion will be reported. At the same time, one should not be astonished by the detailed account of the facts in common law decisions nor by the accurate consideration of previous cases, in contrast, for instance, with the French judicial style. French judgments are very short, they are drafted in a sharp bureaucratic way and they contain generic references to the facts, without any consideration of previous cases (minor changes to this way of drafting were recently introduced, not modifying the substance). Other civil law jurisdictions do not adopt the same approach, which, after all, has recently been questioned in France as well. Therefore, it is important to be aware that many differences continue to exist between common law and civil law judicial styles.[11]

1.6 Contents

Moving finally to illustrate the structure of this book, Chapter 2 is dedicated to the sources of contract law: in the civil law tradition the main rules and principles are to be found in the civil codes, but in the common law countries the structure of contract law is mostly based on case law. From an international point of view, the role of 'soft law' is not to be neglected, with specific

11 For a general overview, see D. N. MacCormick, R. S. Summers (eds.), *Interpreting Precedents. A Comparative Study*, Routledge, London, 1997. About the reforms implemented in France, E. Calzolaio, 'La Corte di cassazione francese abbandona gli *attendus que:* verso un nuovo "stile delle sentenze"?', *Foro it.*, 2019, V, p. 315.

regard to the Unidroit Principles of International Contracts Law and to the European Principles of Contract Law. Chapter 3 deals with the problem of definition of contract, enlightening the role of the will of the parties and the basis for enforcement, with a focus on variation of contracts and on firm offers. Chapter 4 illustrates the formation of contracts and considers the issue of the 'battle of forms', which is debated in the field of international contracts. Chapter 5 considers the theme of precontractual negotiations, showing the different approaches in civil law and common law experiences. Chapter 6 is dedicated to the rules concerning the interpretation of contract, closely connected with the different conceptions of contract in the two legal traditions. Chapter 7 focuses on the relevance of mistake, both when the parties misunderstand the terms of the contract and when communication errors occur. Chapter 8 briefly illustrates the rules concerning the failure to perform the contractual obligations (breach) and it also deals with the controversial topic of penalty clauses, which are in principle not admitted in English law, in contrast with the civil law approach. Chapter 9 discusses the topic of supervening events, presenting the traditional rules, together with some remarks about their adequacy in the light of the problems that emerged during the Covid-19 pandemic. Chapter 10, the last chapter, considers the Vienna Convention on the International Sale of Goods, given its importance and diffusion all over the world with the significant exception of the United Kingdom who never ratified it.

2 The sources of contract law

In the civil law tradition, the general principles and the doctrinal structure of contract law lie on the civil codes provisions. This observation remains true, notwithstanding that the traditional centrality of codes has been progressively eroded by the enactment of many statutes, affecting both specific areas of contract law (such as, for instance, consumer contracts) and certain types of contracts (sale of goods, agency, etc.). In contrast, in the common law tradition, given the absence of codes, the 'general part' of contract law continues to be a combination of rules and principles predominantly based on case law. This being the traditional way of introducing the topic of the sources of contract law, it needs now to be clarified in more detail.

2.1 Civil law: the meaning of code

It is important not to take for granted what a code is. Sometimes, it is assumed that a code is simply a set of rules put in a statutory form. In reality, it is much more than this.

Very briefly, the word code comes from the Latin 'codex', which meant a book that is bound, in contrast with 'volumen', which meant a scroll. The word 'codex' identified a format, rather than a content. Its legal meaning emerged gradually, hand in hand with the use of the word by public authorities (e.g. the Emperors), when they wanted to issue a collection of statutes to be kept for a long time. In this way, the meaning of the word shifted from a format to the content itself and it indicated a collection of statutes and rules, ordered in a coherent way.

DOI: 10.4324/9781003251606-2

The modern meaning of code goes far beyond this. As a consequence of the will theories laid down by Hobbes and then by Von Pufendorf in the 17th century and later by other eminent philosophers, law came to be conceived as the product of the will of the supreme authority, expressed through statutes. In this context, with the French Revolution the idea that predominated in the civil law tradition was to substitute all the ancient rules (the *ius commune*) with a single civil code that aimed to embrace the entire field of private law, destined to become the sole source of (private) law. The French civil code was conceived as a text of legal rules enacted by the legislator, covering the entire private law sector, destined to be long lasting, creating entirely new rules that could not be interpreted or integrated with recourse to the previous ones. This conception prevailed at least until the first half of the 20th century. After the Second World War, the explosion of legislation submerged the (at least assumed) unity of the law, undermining the centrality of the civil codes.

Each country has its own civil code. However, the French and German codes strongly influenced all the others. The French code was enacted in 1804 and it is still in force now, notwithstanding the reform of many of its articles. The most recent and important one is the 2016 reform of the law of obligations and contracts. The German code (BGB) was enacted in 1896 and has been in force since 1 January 1900. As in France, it has been amended. The most remarkable reform concerning the law of contracts was enacted in 2002.

Although the civil codes are the primary source of contract law in the civil law tradition, the role of case law should not be underestimated. The code rules are often vague, formulated in abstract ways so that only through their concrete application is it possible to understand their meaning.

2.2 The absence of codification in the common law tradition

In England the codification movement found many supporters, attracted by the idea of encapsulating the dispersive common law rules in single legislative documents. However, the reaction by the defenders of the common law legal tradition was clear-cut. For example, at the beginning of the 19th century, Edward Sugden, a future Lord Chancellor, wrote an incisive reply to the proposal for a code of English real property law:

> In regard to the proposed Code generally, I must avow myself decidedly opposed to *all* codes. The laws owe much to the reverence which their antiquity inspires; and where, as in our case, they have in succession of ages been adapted to the free institutions of the country, it were rash, as the Code proposes, to abolish them all by one declaration, and establish a new law. *Time mellows and indeed forms laws.*[1]

This traditionalistic view prevailed. Even nowadays English contract law continues to be uncodified and essentially case law based. This does not mean that statutory provisions do not affect many contract rules. Rather, it simply means that the main doctrines do not have a statutory origin and basis, but a judicial one. They are built on some core 'precedents' and they cannot be described without a precise reference to their facts: "The law of contract so far as its general principles are concerned has been happily free from legislative interference: it is the product of the vigorous common sense of English judges".[2] An eminent scholar made this statement more than 150 years ago and it continues to be true. The increasing relevance of legislation affects special contracts and all the matters covered by EU Law, especially in consumer protection. However, common law (including equity) still provides the fundamental rules governing all aspects of the law applicable to contracts generally.

2.3 The role of Restatements in the United States

As far as the situation in the United States is concerned, it is useful to remember that contract law is not under federal competence. Consequently, the most important sources of contract law are state case law and state statutes, though there are also many federal statutes governing how contracts are made by and with the federal government.

Especially since the early twentieth century, a large number of contract disputes have been submitted to the courts for resolution, and the published opinions, if collected in one place, would fill dozens of bookshelves. In order

1 E. B. Sugden, *A Letter to James Humphreys, Esq: On His Proposal to Repeal the Laws of Real Property and Substitute a New Code*, 2nd ed., J&WT Clarke, London, 1826, p. 5 (emphasis added).

2 W. Anson, *Principles of the English Law of Contract and of Agency in Relation to Contract*, 1st ed., Clarendon Press, Oxford, 1879, Preface.

to react to the dispersive consequences of such a situation, a group of prominent American judges, lawyers and law teachers founded the American Law Institute (ALI) in 1923, with the aim of clarifying, simplifying and improving the law. One of the ALI's first projects, and ultimately one of its most successful, was the drafting of the Restatement of the Law of Contracts, completed in 1932. A revision – the Restatement (Second) of Contracts – was undertaken in 1964 and completed in 1979. Hereafter, we will often refer to the Restatement (Second) of Contract.

What is a Restatement? The Restatements are detailed analyses of the decided cases, drafted with an eye to discerning the various principles that have emerged from the courts and another eye to outlining the best solutions adopted.[3] To the maximum extent possible, the Restatements declare the law as the courts have determined it to be. Guided by a reporter (the director of the project) and a staff of legal scholars, the drafting processes go through several so-called tentative drafts –sometimes as many as 15 or 20 – and are screened by various committees within the ALI before they are eventually published as final documents.

The Restatements are not statutes and so they are not binding. However, their rules and solutions have a strong unifying effect. They influence the case law of the states' courts, helping to achieve uniformity of the law in the United States. In particular, the Restatement (Second) of Contracts is cited in innumerable cases and it is generally respected and followed by the courts.[4]

It is important to point out that some rules on contract, especially those concerning contracts for the sale of goods, are governed by the Uniform Commercial Code (UCC). In short, until the first decades of the 20th century, the law on sales of goods, negotiable instruments, warehouse receipts, securities and on other matters crucial to doing business in an industrial market economy varied, sometimes greatly, from state to state. In order to react to this situation, the ALI and the National Conference of Commissioners on Uniform State Laws involved the efforts of hundreds of practising lawyers, law teachers and judges to draft a model code, whose final version was published in 1951 and subsequently adopted by legislatures in all fifty states, the District of Columbia, and the American territories. It consists of nine

3 Besides the one on contract law, many other Restatements exist in the fields of torts, agency, conflicts of laws, judgments, property, restitution, security and trusts.

4 For a general overview, cf. G. E. Maggs, 'Ipse Dixit: The Restatement (Second) of Contracts and the Modern Development of Contract Law', *GEO. Wash. L. REV.* 1998, 66, p. 508.

major substantive articles: Article 1: General Provisions; Article 2: Sales; Article 2A: Leases; Article 3: Commercial Paper; Article 4: Bank Deposits and Collections; Article 4A: Funds Transfers; Article 5: Letters of Credit; Article 6: Bulk Transfers; Article 7: Warehouse Receipts, Bills of Lading and Other Documents of Title; Article 8: Investment Securities; Article 9: Secured Transactions.

2.4 International sources: the role of 'soft' law

The differences between contract laws create major problems in international trade. A very important contribution towards unification comes from international conventions. The most important one is the Vienna Convention on International Sales of Goods (CISG), which we will consider in the last chapter.

However, there are also other international initiatives favouring harmonization. Both the UNIDROIT Principles and the Principles of European Contract Law are 'soft laws', in the sense that they are not binding, not being imposed by a public authority. Notwithstanding the absence of a formal value, they play an important role and they are constantly referred to not only in international judicial or arbitration proceedings, but also in domestic cases. As we will consider the solutions provided by these texts while dealing with the specific issues covered in this book, it is important to give some general information about them.

In particular, in 1980 the International Institute for the Unification of Private Law (UNIDROIT) established an intergovernmental working group of contract law experts from a variety of domestic legal systems to prepare the UNIDROIT Principles of International Commercial Contracts (in short: UNIDROIT Principles). The group's objective was to develop internationally agreed principles of contract law to provide a framework for commercial contracts, which would be acceptable to parties from different legal systems.

The UNIDROIT Principles cover contract formation, content, interpretation, performance and remedies as well as matters relating to third party rights, assignment and limitation periods. The core principles are party autonomy, *favor contractus* (i.e. preference for interpretations that will lead to the continuation and fulfilment of the contract rather than to termination), good faith and fair dealing. They are gaining influence in both the international and domestic contracting spheres and have influenced reforms of domestic contract law in a number of jurisdictions.

The Preamble clarifies their main uses. First, they "shall be applied when the parties have agreed that their contract be governed by them". This means that when the parties decide to adopt voluntarily the UNIDROIT Principles to regulate their contract, then judges and arbitrators will have to apply them. Second, they "may be applied when the parties have agreed that their contract be governed by general principles of law, the *lex mercatoria* or the like". Actually, the UNIDROIT Principles often fix rules commonly followed in the field of international contracts so that they can provide for a useful guide to ascertain them. Third, they "may be applied when the parties have not chosen any law to govern their contract" or fourth, they "may be used to interpret or supplement international uniform law instruments". Last, they may be used to interpret or supplement domestic law and they also may serve "as a model for the national and international legislator".

Similarly, the existence of significant differences between contract laws of the (now) 27 member states of the EU was considered to be an obstacle to the development of a truly seamless internal market in Europe. A number of measures have been taken to address this problem. The EU issued minimum harmonization directives establishing baseline requirements for all member states for certain types of contracts (such as consumer credit contracts) and in certain areas of contract law (such as unfair terms).

More ambitiously, the European Commission sponsored the creation of a Draft Common Frame of Reference (DCFR). Published in 2009, this six-volume work contains model European rules of private law with a particular focus on contract law. Some argued that the DCFR would form the basis for a future European Civil Code, although such a project encountered significant resistances and now it seems to have been abandoned.[5]

One of the most interesting achievements is a project which gave rise to the Principles of European Contract Law (PECL). Article 1:101 sets out the general rules regarding the application of the Principles. Similarly to the

5 In October 2011 the European Commission proposed an opt-in Common European Sales Law. The Sales Law would exist in parallel to parties' domestic systems of contract law and would apply to cross-border sales contracts where the parties agree to its application. Although the law as proposed would only be applicable for contracts for the sale of goods, the content of the law would include general contract law rules as well as specific sales-related provisions. Potentially the Sales Law could be extended to other types of contracts and perhaps evolve into a general European contract law. However, the proposal has been withdrawn and this shows the difficulties in moving forward the process of harmonization of private law in Europe.

UNIDROIT Principles, PECL "will apply when the parties have agreed to incorporate them into their contract or that their contract is to be governed by them" and they may be applied when the parties (i) have agreed that their contract is to be governed by "general principles of law", the "lex mercatoria" or the like; (ii) or they have not chosen any system or rules of law to govern their contract. The PECL may also "provide a solution to the issue raised where the system or rules of law applicable do not do so".

3 Promise and contract

3.1 The problem of definition of contract

In the civil law tradition every discourse about contract always starts with its definition. Beyond the differences in the various codes, contract is almost unanimously defined as an 'agreement' having a patrimonial character that the law will enforce provided that the consent between the parties is genuine and that some requirements are fulfilled.

In contrast, in the common law world doctrinal works settle the issue of definition of contract quickly and with some awkwardness, just to introduce the topic and then move on to describe the main rules and principles. Moreover, at least two competing definitions of contract are used in the common law legal systems: i) "an agreement giving rise to obligations which are enforced or recognised by law" and ii) "a promise or a set of promises which the law will enforce".

While neither courts nor parties to contracts describe the relationships that they create in terms of promises, but rather in terms of agreement, the definition of contract as promise tends to be preferred. The idea that contract is an agreement was introduced into English legal discussions only in the 19th century, under the influence of continental writers (such as Pothier). It became of quite common usage during the 20th century, but in recent times it tends to be less used because it does not fit with the traditional common law rules on contract. Significantly, the American Second Restatement of Contracts defines contract as "a promise or a set of promises for the breach of which the law gives a remedy or the performance of which the law in some way recognizes as a duty" (§ 1). This definition is

DOI: 10.4324/9781003251606-3

undoubtedly quite strange for a civil law lawyer, because for him, contract is agreement, not promise.[1]

It is not useful to illustrate the historical evolution of the different approaches to contract in the two legal traditions. Suffice it to notice that, if now we take for granted that a promise can give rise to an enforceable obligation, the history of each legal system shows that it has been a slow and difficult process.[2] What are the conditions or requisites necessary for a promise to produce an obligation? Is the so-called 'bare consent' enough?

Primitive answers to these questions considered that promises could be enforced only if made in the context of specific formalities, having a magic or even religious character. Alternatively, the breach of a promise was seen as a delict (fraud, deceit, trespass, etc.), giving rise to remedies in tort. In short, in every legal system the main problem to tackle has always been to ascertain when a promise is binding.

Roman jurists were not interested in the problem of 'why' an obligation arises from a legal point of view. Rather, they concentrated their attention on 'how' it arises, considering that an agreement is not enough to give rise to an action. *Ex nudo pacto actio non nascitur*: the agreement needs to be 'clothed', and not 'naked'. This 'clothing' is either a specific form through which the agreement has to be reached and expressed, or the presence of a typical contractual scheme (for instance: sale of goods). In the Roman experience, a bare promise is not relevant for the law, with the sole exception of 'vows' or promises to give a reward.

This scenario changes radically between the 12th and 13th centuries as a consequence of the contribution of theologians such as Thomas Aquinas, who preached the moral need to keep promises: if one does not uphold his promise, he lies; if he lies he is a sinner and so he compromises his soul. In later developments, the idea, which also entered the legal discourse, is that a promise generates a reliance on the other party and needs to be protected.

1 For a general overview, see T. J. Schoenbaum, *The Law and Legal System of the United States*, West Academic Publishing, St. Paul, 2016, p. 815 ff.

2 For an in-depth and full account, the inevitable reference is to the seminal work of the distinguished Italian comparatist G. Gorla, 'Il contratto. Problemi fondamentali trattati con il metodo comparativo e casistico', in *Lineamenti generali*, vol. I, Giuffrè, Milan, 1955, p. 2 ff.

In this way, the idea itself of contract tends to be drawn towards the field of promise.

This relationship is subverted in the 17th and 18th centuries, with the Enlightenment theories and particularly with the will theory, according to which *solus consensus obligat* (simple consent generates obligations). Grotius, the founder of the natural school of law, is considered to be at the origin of this principle, even if his works are not so clear in this respect.[3] However, without any doubt the 18th century French writers Domat and Pothier develop the idea that contracts originate from one's will. Every person is free and this freedom means that every person can exercise his will and generate obligations, enforced by the law. In parallel with the development of these ideas, in the civil law world the term 'promise' is confined to the moral sphere. A contractual obligation can arise only if the parties want to be bound. The principle of consent, conceived as the 'meeting of wills', is seen as the main basis of a contract.[4]

In contrast, in English legal history, contract law evolved in a different way.[5] In the early common law (11th–14th century) one could sue on a contract only if there was an appropriate writ. The system based on the forms of action confined the enforceability of promises only if they were contained in documents under seal or if 'something' was given in exchange. The writ of covenant was available against a person whose promise was contained in a sealed deed. The borrower of money could use the writ of debt in order to obtain repayment from the promisor. A general claim for damages for breach of contract emerged only from the law of torts, through the writ of trespass. Originally, this writ covered situations where the defendant had damaged the plaintiff's person or property by force and against the King's peace. Subsequently, its field of application was extended to cover all cases of misperformance of contractual undertakings. As a result, the main rules on liability for breach of contract evolved from an 'extra-contractual' cause of action. This explains, among other aspects, the origin of some rules that will be dealt with in Chapter 8.

3 See G. Gorla, op. cit., p. 46 ff.

4 For an in-depth account of the theory of pure consent cf. the English version of some chapters of Gorla's work *Il contratto*, recently published: G. Gorla, *I problemi fondamentali del contratto*, ESI, Naples, 2017, p. 83 ff., showing that in practice in the civil law systems pure consent is never a source of obligation.

5 See L. Moccia, 'Contract', in *Enc. Giur. Treccani*, vol. V, Rome, 1988.

3.2 The role of will: subjective vs objective

Without going into further details, in light of the above it is intuitive that from the common law perspective the promisor's will to be bound and the promisee's will to accept (the 'meeting of minds', in the continental meaning of this expression) are not relevant in themselves. Rather, the idea of contract is built on promise and, in particular, on the protection of the promisee's reliance. Under the influence of legal rationalism (which spread in Europe in the 18th century), the will theory started to be well known in England. Consequently, the terminology sometimes changed. However, the substance of the traditional approach is still predominant and the will theory was never accepted.

In the common law experience, contracts tend to be restricted only to the exchange of onerous promises. Neither gifts nor agreements formed through delivery (for instance, the rent-free lease) are contracts, in contrast with the civil law tradition.

From these premises, traditionally comparatists emphasize a sharp distinction. The civil law follows a subjective approach, according to which the creation of the contract requires that the parties actually intend the same thing. The common law tends to privilege an objective approach, giving relevance to what a reasonable person could objectively infer from the declarations or the conduct of the other party.

In reality, as we will discuss, the distinction is much more nuanced and should not be overestimated: on the one hand, it is not true that the intention always prevails in the continental legal tradition; on the other, it is inaccurate to state that the parties' intentions are never relevant in the common law tradition.

Some examples will help to become more familiar with the way judges reason in the two legal traditions.

The English case *Paal Wilson & Co. v Partenreederei* is illustrative of the common law objective approach: "what is necessary is that the intention as it has been communicated to and understood by the other (even though that which has been communicated does not represent the actual state of mind of the communicator) should coincide".[6]

This case concerns a contract where the parties agreed on the sale of a vessel. A dispute arose, as the buyers notified the sellers that they had a claim

6 *Paal Wilson & Co. v Partenreederei* [1983] 1 A.C. 854.

against them in respect of the speed of the ship, and the sellers rejected this claim. The contract contained an arbitration clause. Arbitration proceedings started in 1972, but they were pursued only sporadically and neither party did anything for many years. Only in 1980, did the buyer ask for a date to be fixed for the hearing. The seller claimed that the arbitration agreement had been frustrated so that neither party had either the duty or the right to proceed further with the reference, and that, if either should wish to do so, he should be restrained by injunction from so acting. The High Court and the Court of Appeal held that the agreement had been frustrated by the delay of both the parties. The House of Lords reversed this decision.

It is a very long case and we will report only some parts of it, in order to catch the judges' way of reasoning.

Lord Diplock

[…] Abandonment of a contract ("the former contract") which is still executory, i.e., one in which at least one primary obligation of one or other of the parties remains unperformed, is effected by the parties entering into a new contract ("the contract of abandonment") by which each party promises the other to release that other party from further performance of any primary obligations on his part under the former contract then remaining unperformed, but without such non-performance giving rise to any substituted secondary obligation under the former contract to pay damages.

It is the latter part of the promise by each party, i.e., the release of the other party from all further secondary as well as primary obligations, that distinguishes the legal concept of abandonment of the former contract from the extinction of unperformed primary obligations of both parties under the former contract by fundamental breach of a primary obligation (or breach of condition) by one of them, followed by the election of the party not in breach to put an end to all primary obligations of both parties under the former contract remaining unperformed. Unlike the contract of abandonment this leaves the secondary obligations under the former contract of the party who committed the breach enforceable against him by the other party.

To the formation of the contract of abandonment, the ordinary principles of the English law of contract apply. To create a contract by exchange of promises between two parties where the promise of each party constitutes the consideration for the promise of the other, *what is necessary is that the intention of each as it has been communicated to and understood by the other (even though that which has been communicated does not represent the actual state of mind of the communicator) should coincide*. That is what English lawyers mean when they resort to the Latin phrase consensus ad idem and the words that I have italicised are essential to the concept of consensus ad idem, the lack of which prevents the formation of a binding contract in English law.

Thus if A (the offeror) makes a communication to B (the offeree) whether in writing, orally or by conduct, which, in the circumstances at the time the communication was received, (1) B, if he were a reasonable man, would understand as stating A's intention to act or refrain from acting in some specified manner if B will promise on his part to act or refrain from acting in some manner also specified in the offer, and (2) B does in fact understand A's communication to mean this, and in his turn makes to A a communication conveying his willingness so to act or to refrain from acting [...] the consensus ad idem essential to the formation of a contract in English law is complete.

The rule that neither party can rely upon his own failure to communicate accurately to the other party his own real intention by what he wrote or said or did, as negativing the consensus ad idem, is an example of a general principle of English law that injurious reliance on what another person did may be a source of legal rights against him. I use the broader expression "injurious reliance" in preference to "estoppel" so as to embrace all circumstances in which A can say to B: "You led me reasonably to believe that you were assuming particular legally enforceable obligations to me," of which promissory or High Trees estoppel [*Central London Property Trust Ltd. v. High Trees House Ltd.* [1947] K.B. 130] affords another example; whereas "estoppel," in the strict sense of the term, is an exclusionary rule of evidence, though it may operate so as to affect substantive legal rights inter partes.

In the instant case, as in most cases where abandonment of a former contract is relied on, the contract of abandonment of the arbitration agreement is said by the sellers to have been created by the conduct of the parties, consisting of their common inaction, after the buyers' letter of December 12, 1979. Where the inference that a reasonable man would draw from the prolonged failure by the claimant in an arbitration procedure is that the claimant is willing to consent to the abandonment of the agreement to submit the dispute to arbitration and the respondent did in fact draw such inference and by his own inaction thereafter indicated his own consent to its abandonment in similar fashion to the claimant and was so understood by the claimant, the court would be right in treating the arbitration agreement as having been terminated by abandonment. In *André et Compagnie S.A. v. Marine Transocean Ltd. (The Splendid Sun)* [1981] Q.B. 694, all three members of the Court of Appeal drew such an inference from the conduct of both parties in the arbitration. That case was, in my view, rightly decided, though not for reasons other than those which were given by Eveleigh and Fox L.JJ.

The facts in the instant case, however, are very different from those of *The Splendid Sun*. As my noble and learned friends,

Lord Brandon of Oakbrook and Lord Brightman, both point out, they *are inconsistent with any actual belief on the part of the sellers that the buyers had agreed to abandon the arbitration before their letter of July 30, which stated their intention of continuing with it.*

Your Lordships were urged to hold that the absence of any actual belief on the part of the sellers did not matter so long as someone in the sellers' position could not unreasonably have drawn the inference from the apparent inaction of the buyers that they had abandoned the arbitration at some date between their letter of December 12, 1979, when they were manifestly treating the arbitration as being still alive, and July 30, 1980, when they wrote to the sellers forwarding their expert's report and asking for a hearing date for the arbitration to be fixed. The absence of actual belief on the sellers' part that the buyers had abandoned the arbitration, however, would mean that there had in fact been no injurious reliance by the sellers; and to treat that ingredient of consensus ad idem as unnecessary would introduce into the law of contract a novel heresy which your Lordships should, in my view, be vigilant to reject.

Applying the orthodox concept of termination of contract by abandonment, neither the trial judge nor any member of the Court of Appeal was prepared to hold that the sellers were entitled to succeed on this ground; and even if your Lordships yourselves felt some doubt upon this issue, which I myself do not, I agree with my noble and learned friends that your Lordships would hesitate long before upsetting the unanimous decision of the judges in the lower courts on what, upon a proper application of the law of contract, is essentially a question of fact.

Lord Brightman

[...] The basis of "tacit abandonment by both parties," to use the phraseology of the sellers' case is that the primary facts are such that it ought to be inferred that the contract to arbitrate the particular dispute was rescinded by the mutual agreement of the parties. To entitle the sellers to rely on abandonment, they must show that the buyers so conducted themselves as to entitle the sellers to assume, and that the sellers did assume, that the contract was agreed to be abandoned sub silentio. The evidence which is relevant to that inquiry will consist of or include: (1) What the buyers did or omitted to do to the knowledge of the sellers. Excluded from consideration will be the acts of the buyers of which the sellers were ignorant, because those acts will have signalled nothing to the sellers and cannot have founded or fortified any assumption on the part of the sellers. (2) What the sellers did or omitted to do, whether or not to the knowledge of the buyers. These facts evidence the state of mind of the sellers, and therefore the validity of the assertion by the sellers that they assumed that the contract was agreed to be abandoned. The state of mind of the buyers is irrelevant to a consideration of what the sellers were entitled to assume. The state of mind of the sellers is vital to a consideration of what the sellers in fact assumed.

In the instant case there is a period of 21 months which contains the acts and omissions relied upon by the sellers. During that period there were five communications from buyers to sellers. Those communications can be relied upon by the buyers to counter the submission that the sellers were entitled to assume that the contract to arbitrate had been abandoned by the buyers. There were during the same period four additional acts on the part of the buyers inconsistent with an intention on their part to rescind the arbitration agreement, of which the sellers were ignorant. The buyers cannot rely on those acts. Per contra,

> there were two important steps taken by the sellers, without the knowledge of the buyers, inconsistent with the proposition that the sellers assumed the arbitration was abandoned. This evidence, though going to the state of mind of the sellers and signalling nothing to the buyers, is admissible and in the instant case decisive.

In contrast, according to the French approach, if one party said something but intended something different, there is no agreement at all.

A French case is useful to show this approach.[7] It deals with a contract of sale of a large quantity of wine produced in Algeria and to be delivered to Cherchell (a town on the Algerian coast). The buyers wanted the wine to be delivered in Algiers and offered to share the cost of transport. The sellers demanded the sum of 60 francs per hectolitre and the buyers counteroffered 30 francs, but in fact they wrote 300 francs instead of 30. The sellers, of course, immediately accepted, they delivered the wine and billed the buyers accordingly. After the payment, the buyers realized their mistake and demanded repayment. The Cour d'appel of Montpellier gave judgment for the buyers. The sellers unsuccessfully appealed.

> Whereas the statements in the contested judgment show that [the seller Tirat] was obliged to deliver 2.000 hectolitres of Algerian wine FOB[8] to the purchasers [Orazzi] and that the delivery would have taken place at Cherchell, which [the purchasers] refused, offering to share the cost of haulage from Cherchell to Algiers;
>
> That this offer was set out in a telegram agreeing to pay 300 francs a hectolitre;

7 Court of Cassation, ch. comm., 15 February 1961. The original text is freely accessible through the following link: www.legifrance.gouv.fr/juri/id/JURITEXT000006956670/. The translation in English is provided by the author.

8 FOB (free on board) is a term defined in the INCOTERMS. It means that the seller is responsible for transportation of the goods to the port of shipment and the cost of loading. The risk of perishment passes to the buyer when the goods are loaded at the port of origin.

That after acceptance and delivery, [the purchasers] claimed that the figure of 300 francs was the result of material error and that the true figure was 30 francs; as the sum was calculated on the basis of the first figure, [the purchasers] issued a bill of exchange on [the buyer] for the amount of 335,162, which was dishonoured and protested;

Whereas [the seller] then sued [the purchasers] for damages for the loss caused by a bill of exchange improperly presented and then protested, whereupon [the purchasers] counter-claimed for payment of the bill; subsequently the court of first instance recognized in its contested judgment that a mistake had been made and dismissed the claim in the main proceedings and upheld [the purchaser's] counterclaim;

Whereas the appellant challenges the judgment inasmuch as it declared that the agreement as to haulage charges was invalid by reason of a substantial mistake, because it incorrectly showed the sum of 300 francs instead of 30 francs, whereas, the appellant argues: first, a mistake as to the value is not a material mistake and in any event the court failed to explain its reasoning concerning the claims made by [the seller] on that point; second, a voidable act is valid until a court declares that it is void and consequently the bill of exchange lacked a legal basis, having been presented before any annulment; finally, the contested judgment ascertained that [the purchaser] had confirmed the contract by accepting, without any contestation, the agreement reached on the offer of 300 francs and the accounts presented, so that it was possible for the court to remedy the curable nullity arising from a mistake;

Whereas, however, it is stated in the judgment that, for the reasons set out, the figure of 300 francs per hectolitre in [the purchaser's] telegram could only be the result of a material mistake; *as [the purchaser] proposed or believed it was proposing 30 francs, that is to say half of what [the seller] asked for;*

therefore no agreement was reached as to the amount; due to this diverging of wills, being the result of a misunderstanding, no agreement had been reached[9]; accordingly, on the one side, the court, did not have to declare the contract void for a mistake as to the characteristics of its object and was not required to answer any arguments put forward to this point; on the other side, having found that no agreement had been concluded concerning the division of haulage costs, the court could not find that there was no legal basis for the bill of exchange which was based on market terms and the abovementioned offer of 30 francs. [...]

On these grounds, the Court dismisses the appeal against the judgment of the Cour d'appel of Montpellier of 16 October 1957.

3.3 Basis for enforcement: cause and consideration

All legal systems have to face the problem of selecting which promises or agreements are legally binding. No one doubts that a promise or a declaration in a familial context or between friends in a pub is not binding.

3.3.1 Civil law

In the civil law tradition, the issue outlined above is traditionally addressed recurring to the notion of cause (causa). The medieval canonists (i.e. experts in the law of the Church) considered that a promise was binding if it was made *serio et deliberato animo*, that is to say with the intention of being bound by it. The effectiveness of this intention was ensured by the presence of a 'sufficient reason', the lack of which made the promise ineffective. Some scholars suggest that the *animus obligandi* (the intention to be bound) was essential because of the commandment to tell the truth: it was a sin to break

9 Emphasis added.

one's promise, except when the promisor had no intention at all of being bound by it. The doctrine of *cause* meant that every promise binds if it is made deliberately and for a licit aim.

As mentioned before, from the 17th century onwards the contribution of the school of natural law developed the idea of the creative power of will, affirming that even a bare promise (*nudo pactum*) is enough to create a contract. This principle inspired the 19th century's codification process. For instance, the French civil code of 1804 clearly makes the validity of a contract dependent on its having an underlying cause. According to Article 1108 (now reformed), four requisites were essential for the validity of an agreement: consent of the party who binds himself; his capacity to contract; a definite object which forms the subject-matter of the undertaking; and a lawful cause in the obligation.

Torrents of learned ink have been spilt on the true nature of cause. The real meaning and use of this concept is difficult to grasp.[10] Sometimes, the term is used in order to affirm that a contract is void when it is contrary to good morals, when it is contrary to the law or when it is based on an illicit cause. In these cases, cause denotes the totality of the aims pursued by the parties on entering the contract in question. In other circumstances, cause denotes essentially the counter performance, whose absence renders the contract void. For example, assume that a person promises to pay the operator of a driving school for the transfer of the operating license: if such a license can be obtained merely by applying to the authorities and satisfying the normal conditions, there is absence of cause, because the counter performance of the promise to pay is valueless.

A French case is useful to illustrate the role of cause.[11] According to a well-established banking practice, customer remittances are not entered immediately, but only after a certain period of time, whereas payments from the account by the bank (debits) are entered with a date preceding the date of the transaction. As a result, the calculation of interest is charged from the date on which the credit or debit is entered. In the following case, the French Cour de cassation considers that this practice is not legal: according to the (then) Art. 1131, any transaction is void if cause is lacking.

10 Cf. G. Gorla, *I problemi fondamentali* etc., p. 49 ff.

11 Cass. Com., 6 April 1993. The original text is freely accessible through the following link: www.legifrance.gouv.fr/juri/id/JURITEXT000007030513/. The translation in English is provided by the author.

> Whereas according to the judgment appealed against (Aix-en-Provence, 2nd Civil Chamber, 3 October 1990) the companies [...], which held current accounts with the [Bank], sued the Bank for recovery of fees charged; as the Bank cross-claimed for an order that the companies should pay to it the amounts debited to their account. [...]
>
> Whereas the companies claimed that their obligation to pay interest was in part unsupported by any cause, inasmuch as the amounts on which interest was calculated were increased, without justification, by the application of "dates of valuation" to remittances in the form of cheques and cash and to the withdrawals;
>
> Whereas in rejecting that claim, the lower court found that the practice adopted by the Bank and contested by the companies was justified by the fact that "a remittance for the credit on an account, like a withdrawal debited to an account, takes time to collect or pay out", and that "the value of a cheque can be credited to an account only after collection which cannot be instantaneous";
>
> Whereas by so holding, whilst the transactions at issue [...] did not involve the postponement or bringing forward of the dates on which such amounts were to be credited or debited, not even for the purpose of calculating interest, the cour d'appel infringed the abovementioned provision.
>
> On those grounds the judgment is quashed and the case referred to the cour d'appel of Lyon.

Quite surprisingly, the requisite of cause was abolished by the recent French reform of obligations and contracts. However, some French scholars argue that it remains an essential pillar of the law of contract. Italian law (Art. 1325) and Spanish law (Art. 1261) both follow the (original) French model.

German law has never used cause as a basis of the validity of contract. However, the issues classified as failure of cause or as false cause according to the original French model are solved recurring to the doctrine of unjust enrichment. Heavily inspired by Roman law, the relevant rules on unjust enrichment are described in the book on obligations (§§ 812–822) and they are generally applicable in every field of private law. § 812 BGB states as follows:

> A person who obtains something as a result of the performance of another person or otherwise at his expense without legal grounds for doing so is under a duty to make restitution to him. This duty also applies if the legal grounds later lapse or if the result intended to be achieved by those efforts in accordance with the contents of the legal transaction does not occur.[12]

3.3.2 Common law

English law has never made recourse to cause, but to consideration, which is one of the most elusive and debated doctrines. The word emerged during the first half of the 16th century, where it was used by the Court of Chancery (so in the field of equity), under the influence of the civil law concept of *causa promissionis*. Little by little, the term began to be used also in the common law courts. The first case is *Sharington v Strotton* of 1565, reported by Plowden, published in Law French in 1571 and translated into English in 1761. It concerned the conveyance of land by 'use' (the ancestor of trust) by the owner to his brother and heirs, reserving a life interest (a liferent). The case arose on a writ of trespass against Strotton and others for taking timber without authority from land subject to a 'use' contained in a deed. The crucial issue was whether the 'use' was valid. Counsel for the plaintiffs argued that it was invalid since there was no consideration. Plowden argued that it was valid since a deed 'imported consideration', a proposition of law accepted by later courts and one which still prevails today. The word 'consideration' was used extensively in the case report (more than 100 times), as a synonym for a 'reason' or 'basis', a 'purpose' or 'motive', a 'price', 'payment', 'recompense' or 'reward'; in 'exchange for' or in 'return for', on 'reflection'. The relevant meaning was an equivalent to 'payment' or 'price':

12 For this translation, cf. G. Dannemann, R. Schulze (eds.), *German Civil Code (BGB), Article-by-Article Commentary*, C.H.Beck-Nomos, Munich, 2020, p. 1578.

> the law has provided that a contract by words shall not bind without consideration [...] As if I promise to give you £20 to make your sale de novo. [...] And *because words are often times spoken by men unadvisedly and without deliberation, the law has provided that a contract by words shall not bind without consideration* [...]. And the reason is, because it is by words which pass from men lightly and inconsiderately, but where the agreement is by deed, there is more time for deliberation. For when a man passes a thing by deed, first there is the determination of the mind to do it, and upon that he causes it to be written, which is one part of deliberation, and afterwards he puts his seal to it, which is another part of deliberation, and lastly he delivers the writing as his deed, which is the consummation of his resolution; and by the delivery of the deed from him that makes it to him to whom it is made, he gives his assent to part with the thing contained in the deed to him to whom he delivers the deed, and this delivery is as a ceremony in law, signifying his good-will that the thing in the deed should pass from him to the other.[13]

In the 18th century, Lord Mansfield unsuccessfully attempted to reduce the requisite of consideration as evidence of the will to assume an obligation, which could be proved also in another way, for instance when the will resulted in writing.[14] The common law courts refused to distinguish between oral and written form and re-established the consideration as an autonomous and necessary element for promises to be binding, except when they were made through a deed.[15] So, despite the initial parallelism with the continental notion of cause, consideration assumed a different scope. It did not refer to the *animus obligandi* (intention to be bound), but to the responsibility of the promisor. For the common lawyers, the *animus* was an insufficient element to be the foundation of a contractual obligation. The doctrine of consideration was founded on the idea that a simple promise is not binding, even if it is legal and accepted by the other party, except if it is supported by a reason that would make it enforceable (or actionable). Again, as mentioned before, this was due essentially to the origins of the rules concerning contract law being gradually developed from extra-contractual remedies (in particular, the

13 1 Plowden's *Commentaries*, 308 [E.R. vol. 75, p. 470].
14 *Pillans v Van Mierop*, 1663, 3 Burrow [E.R. vol. 97, p. 1035].
15 *Rann v Hughes*, 1778, 4 Brown's *Parliamentary Cases*, 27 [E.R. vol. 2, p. 18].

writ of trespass). The selective function of consideration is now reflected in the modern rule according to which only the promises that are part of a bargain are binding.[16]

Many definitions of consideration have been suggested. Pollock talks about "an act of forbearance of the one party, or the promise thereof, is the price for which the promise of the other is bought and the promise thus given for value is enforceable".[17] This definition has been contested,[18] but instead of insisting on an account of the doctrinal debate, it seems more useful to concentrate our attention on some typical situations, showing both the concrete operation of consideration in the common law legal tradition and the differences from the civil law approach.

3.4 The problem of variation of contracts

3.4.1 The English approach

The parties may agree to modify or to terminate an existing contractual promise, either through an 'increasing pact' (a promise by one party to pay more for the other party's services, for example building work) or a 'decreasing pact' (a promise by one party to accept part-payment by the other party as full discharge of his debt). These pacts might be concluded in situations where the obligations to work or to pay will continue to arise after the date of the relevant negotiation (interim pacts) or in situations where the pact is made after the obligation to work or to pay owed by the promise has already arisen in full (final pacts).

For interim and final decreasing pacts a remedy can be envisaged relating to the equity doctrine of promissory estoppel. In case of an interim increasing pact, the case we will consider immediately below shows that practical benefit is considered as sufficient consideration. The most problematic situation concerns final increasing pacts, because a promise to pay more for a job

16 L. Moccia, Contract, cit.

17 F. Pollock, *Principles of Contract : A Treatise on the General Principles Concerning the Validity of Agreements in the Law of England*, 8th ed., Stevens and Sons Ltd., London, 1911, p. 175.

18 For a full account, see. C. Costantini, 'The Unburiable Contract: Grant Gilmore's Discontinuous Parabola and the Literary Construction of American Legal Style', in P.G. Monateri (ed.), *Comparative Contract Law*, Edward Elgar, Cheltenham, 2017, p. 245 ff. and P. Pardolesi, Promissory Estoppel, ivi, p. 469 ff.

already completed would appear to lack consideration and to fall within the scope of the 'past consideration' rule.

The English case *Williams v Roffey Bros and Nicholls (Contractors)* well illustrates the issue of increasing pacts.[19]

The plaintiff entered into a subcontract with the defendants, who held the main building contract, to carry out carpentry work in a block of 27 flats for an agreed price of £20,000. The plaintiff got into financial difficulty because the agreed price was too low for him to operate satisfactorily and at a profit. The main contract contained a time penalty clause and the defendants, worried that the plaintiff did not complete the carpentry work on time, made an oral agreement to pay the plaintiff an additional sum of £10,300 at the rate of £575 for each flat on which the carpentry work had been completed. Approximately seven weeks later, when the plaintiff had substantially completed eight more flats, the defendants had made only one further payment of £1,500 whereupon the plaintiff ceased work on the flats. The plaintiff then sued the defendants for the additional sum promised. The judge held that the agreement for payment of the additional sum was enforceable and did not fail for lack of consideration, and gave judgment for the plaintiff.

Dismissing the appeal, it was held that where a party to a contract promised to make an additional payment in return for the other party's promise to perform his existing contractual obligations and as a result secured a benefit or avoided a detriment, the advantage secured by the promise to make the additional payment was capable of constituting consideration, provided that it was not secured by economic duress or fraud. The defendants' promise to pay the plaintiff the additional sum of £10,300, in return for the plaintiff's promise to perform his existing contractual obligations on time, resulted in a commercial advantage for the defendants. The benefit accruing to the defendants provided sufficient consideration to support the defendants' promise to pay the additional sum. Accordingly, the agreement for payment of the additional sum was enforceable.

19 *Williams v Roffey Bros and Nicholls (Contractors) Ltd* [1990] All ER 512.

Glidewell LJ

Was there consideration for the defendants' promise made on 9 April 1986 to pay an additional price at the rate of £575 per completed flat?

The judge made the following findings of fact which are relevant on this issue. (i) The subcontract price agreed was too low to enable the plaintiff to operate satisfactorily and at a profit. Mr. Cottrell, the defendants' surveyor, agreed that this was so. (ii) Mr. Roffey (managing director of the defendants) was persuaded by Mr. Cottrell that the defendants should pay a bonus to the plaintiff. The figure agreed at the meeting on 9 April 1986 was £10,300.

The judge quoted and accepted the evidence of Mr. Cottrell to the effect that a main contractor who agrees too low a price with a subcontractor is acting contrary to his own interests. He will never get the job finished without paying more money. The judge therefore concluded:

> In my view where the original subcontract price is too low, and the parties subsequently agree that additional moneys shall be paid to the subcontractor, this agreement is in the interests of both parties. This is what happened in the present case, and in my opinion the agreement of 9 April 1986 does not fail for lack of consideration.

In his address to us, Mr. Evans outlined the benefits to his clients, the defendants, which arose from their agreement to pay the additional £10,300 as: (i) seeking to ensure that the plaintiff continued work and did not stop in breach of the subcontract; (ii) avoiding the penalty for delay; and (iii) avoiding the trouble and expense of engaging other people to complete the carpentry work.

However, Mr. Evans submits that, though his clients may have derived, or hoped to derive, practical benefits from their agreement to pay the "bonus," they derived no benefit in law, since the plaintiff was promising to do no more than he was already bound to do by his subcontract, i.e., continue with the carpentry work and complete it on time. Thus there was no consideration for the agreement. Mr. Evans relies on the principle of law which, traditionally, is based on the decision in *Stilk v. Myrick* (1809) 2 Camp. 317. That was a decision at first instance of Lord Ellenborough C.J. On a voyage to the Baltic, two seamen deserted. The captain agreed with the rest of the crew that if they worked the ship back to London without the two seamen being replaced, he would divide between them the pay which would have been due to the two deserters. On arrival at London this extra pay was refused, and the plaintiff's action to recover his extra pay was dismissed. Counsel for the defendant argued that such an agreement was contrary to public policy, but Lord Ellenborough C.J.'s judgment was based on lack of consideration. It reads, at pp. 318–319:

> I think *Harris v. Watson* (1791) Peake 102 was rightly decided; but I doubt whether the ground of public policy, upon which Lord Kenyon is stated to have proceeded, be the true principle on which the decision is to be supported. Here, I say the agreement is void for want of consideration. There was no consideration for the ulterior pay promised to the mariners who remained with the ship. Before they sailed from London they had undertaken to do all they could under all the emergencies of the voyage. They had sold all their services till the voyage should be completed. If they had been at liberty to quit the vessel at Cronstadt, the case would have been quite different; or if the captain had capriciously discharged the two men who were wanting, the others might not have been compellable to take the whole duty upon themselves, and their agreeing to do so might have been a sufficient

> consideration for the promise of an advance of wages. But the desertion of a part of the crew is to be considered an emergency of the voyage as much as their death; and those who remain are bound by the terms of their original contract to exert themselves to the utmost to bring the ship in safety to her destined port. Therefore, without looking to the policy of this agreement, I think it is void for want of consideration, and that the plaintiff can only recover at the rate of £5 a month.

In *North Ocean Shipping Co. Ltd. v. Hyundai Construction Co. Ltd.* [1979] Q.B. 705, Mocatta J. regarded the general principle of the decision in *Stilk v. Myrick*, 2 Camp. 317 as still being good law. He referred to two earlier decision of this court, dealing with wholly different subjects, in which Denning L.J. sought to escape from the confines of the rule, but was not accompanied in his attempt by the other members of the court. In *Ward v. Byham* [1956] 1 W.L.R. 496 the plaintiff and the defendant lived together unmarried for five years, during which time the plaintiff bore their child. After the parties ended their relationship, the defendant promised to pay the plaintiff £1 per week to maintain the child, provided that she was well looked after and happy. The defendant paid this sum for some months, but ceased to pay when the plaintiff married another man. On her suing for the amount due at £1 per week, he pleaded that there was no consideration for his agreement to pay for the plaintiff to maintain her child, since she was obliged by law to do so: see section 42 of the National Assistance Act 1948. The county court judge upheld the plaintiff mother's claim, and this court dismissed the defendant's appeal. Denning L.J. said, at p. 498:

> I approach the case, therefore, on the footing that the mother, in looking after the child, is only doing what she is legally bound to do. Even so, I think that there was

> sufficient consideration to support the promise. I have always thought that a promise to perform an existing duty, or the performance of it, should be regarded as good consideration, because it is a benefit to the person to whom it is given. Take this very case. It is as much a benefit for the father to have the child looked after by the mother as by a neighbour. If he gets the benefit for which he stipulated, he ought to honour his promise; and he ought not to avoid it by saying that the mother was herself under a duty to maintain the child. I regard the father's promise in this case as what is sometimes called a unilateral contract, a promise in return for an act, a promise by the father to pay £1 a week in return for the mother's looking after the child. Once the mother embarked on the task of looking after the child, there was a binding contract. So long as she looked after the child, she would be entitled to £1 a week. The case seems to me to be within the decision of *Hicks v. Gregory* (1849) 8 C.B. 378 on which the judge relied. I would dismiss the appeal.

However, Morris L.J. put it rather differently. He said, at pp. 498–499:

> Mr. Lane submits that there was a duty on the mother to support the child; that no affiliation proceedings were in prospect or were contemplated; and that the effect of the arrangement that followed the letter was that the father was merely agreeing to pay a bounty to the mother. It seems to me that the terms of the letter negative those submissions, for the husband says "providing you can prove that she"—that is Carol—"will be well looked after and happy and also that she is allowed to decide for herself whether or not she wishes to come and live with you." The father goes on to say that Carol is then well and happy and looking much

> stronger than ever before. "If you decide what to do let me know as soon as possible." It seems to me, therefore, that the father was saying, in effect: Irrespective of what may be the strict legal position, what I am asking is that you shall prove that Carol will be well looked after and happy, and also that you must agree that Carol is to be allowed to decide for herself whether or not she wishes to come and live with you. If those conditions were fulfilled the father was agreeable to pay. Upon those terms, which in fact became operative, the father agreed to pay £1 a week. In my judgment, there was ample consideration there to be found for his promise, which I think was binding.

Parker L.J. agreed. As I read the judgment of Morris L.J., he and Parker L.J. held that, though in maintaining the child the plaintiff was doing no more than she was obliged to do by law, nevertheless her promise that the child would be well looked after and happy was a practical benefit to the father which amounted to consideration for his promise.

In *Williams v. Williams* [1957] 1 W.L.R. 148, a wife left her husband, and he promised to make her a weekly payment for her maintenance.

On his failing to honour his promise, the wife claimed the arrears of payment, but her husband pleaded that, since the wife was guilty of desertion she was bound to maintain herself, and thus there was no consideration for his promise. Denning L.J., at p. 151, reiterated his view that:

> a promise to perform an existing duty is, I think, sufficient consideration to support a promise, so long as there is nothing in the transaction which is contrary to the public interest.

However, the other members of the court (Hodson and Morris L.JJ.) declined to agree with this expression of view, though agreeing with Denning L.J. in finding that there was consideration because the wife's desertion might not have been permanent, and thus there was a benefit to the husband. [...]

[T]he present state of the law on this subject can be expressed in the following proposition: (i) if A has entered into a contract with B to do work for, or to supply goods or services to, B in return for payment by B; and (ii) at some stage before A has completely performed his obligations under the contract B has reason to doubt whether A will, or will be able to, complete his side of the bargain; and (iii) B thereupon promises A an additional payment in return for A's promise to perform his contractual obligations on time; and (iv) as a result of giving his promise, B obtains in practice a benefit, or obviates a disbenefit; and (v) B's promise is not given as a result of economic duress or fraud on the part of A; then (vi) the benefit to B is capable of being consideration for B's promise, so that the promise will be legally binding.

As I have said, Mr. Evans accepts that in the present case by promising to pay the extra £10,300 his client secured benefits. There is no finding, and no suggestion, that in this case the promise was given as a result of fraud or duress. If it be objected that the propositions above contravene the principle in *Stilk v. Myrick*, 2 Camp. 317, I answer that in my view they do not; they refine, and limit the application of that principle, but they leave the principle unscathed e.g. where B secures no benefit by his promise. It is not in my view surprising that a principle enunciated in relation to the rigours of seafaring life during the Napoleonic wars should be subjected during the succeeding 180 years to a process of refinement and limitation in its application in the present day. It is therefore my opinion that on his findings of fact in the present case, the judge was entitled to hold, as he did, that the defendants' promise to pay the extra £10,300 was supported by valuable consideration, and thus constituted an enforceable agreement.

As a subsidiary argument, Mr. Evans submits that on the facts of the present case the consideration, even if otherwise good, did not "move from the promisee." This submission is based on the principle illustrated in the decision in *Tweddle v. Atkinson* (1861) 1 B. & S. 393. My understanding of the meaning of the requirement that "consideration must move from the promisee" is that such consideration must be provided by the promisee, or arise out of his contractual relationship with the promisor. It is consideration provided by somebody else, not a party to the contract, which does not "move from the promisee." This was the situation in *Tweddle v. Atkinson*, but it is, of course, not the situation in the present case. Here the benefits to the defendants arose out of their agreement of 9 April 1986 with the plaintiff, the promisee. In this respect I would adopt the following passage from Chitty on Contracts, 26th ed. (1989), p. 126 para. 183, and refer to the authorities there cited:

> The requirement that consideration must move from the promisee is most generally satisfied where some detriment is suffered by him e.g. where he parts with money or goods, or renders services, in exchange for the promise. But the requirement may equally well be satisfied where the promisee confers a benefit on the promisor without in fact suffering any detriment.

That is the situation in this case. I repeat, therefore, my opinion that the judge was, as a matter of law, entitled to hold that there was valid consideration to support the agreement under which the defendants promised to pay an additional £10,300 at the rate of £575 per flat. For these reasons I would dismiss this appeal.

Purchas L.J.

In my judgment, therefore, the rule in *Stilk v. Myrick*, 2 Camp. 317 remains valid as a matter of principle, namely that a contract not under seal must be supported by consideration. Thus, where the agreement upon which reliance is placed provides that an extra payment is to be made for work to be done by the payee which he is already obliged to perform then unless some other consideration is detected to support the agreement to pay the extra sum that agreement will not be enforceable. The two cases, *Harris v. Watson*, Peake 102 and *Stilk v. Myrick*, 2 Camp. 317 involved circumstances of a very special nature, namely the extraordinary conditions existing at the turn of the 18th century under which seamen had to serve their contracts of employment on the high seas. There were strong public policy grounds at that time to protect the master and owners of a ship from being held to ransom by disaffected crews. Thus, the decision that the promise to pay extra wages even in the circumstances established in those cases, was not supported by consideration is readily understandable. Of course, conditions today on the high seas have changed dramatically and it is at least questionable, as Mr. Makey submitted, whether these cases might not well have been decided differently if they were tried today. The modern cases tend to depend more upon the defence of duress in a commercial context rather than lack of consideration for the second agreement. In the present case the question of duress does not arise. The initiative in coming to the agreement of 9 April came from Mr. Cottrell and not from the plaintiff. It would not, therefore, lie in the defendants' mouth to assert a defence of duress. Nevertheless, the court is more ready in the presence of this defence being available in the commercial context to look for mutual advantages which would amount to sufficient consideration to support the second agreement under which the extra money is paid. [...]

[T]he question now must be addressed: Was there evidence upon which the judge was entitled to find that there was sufficient consideration to support the agreement of 9 April, as set out in the passage from his judgment already set out in the judgment of Glidewell L.J.? The references to this problem in Chitty on Contracts 26th ed. (1989), are not wholly without some conflict amongst themselves. In paragraph 1601 the editors turn to the question of consideration to support an agreement to vary an existing contract:

> In many cases, consideration can be found in the mutual abandonment of existing rights or the conferment of new benefits by each party on the other.

Reference is made to the Woodhouse case to which I have already referred:

> For example, an alteration of the money of account in a contract proposed or made by one party and accepted by the other is binding on both parties, since either may benefit from the variation [...] However, an agreement whereby one party undertakes an additional obligation, but the other party is merely bound to perform his existing obligations, or an agreement whereby one party undertakes an additional obligation, but for the benefit of that party alone, will not be effective to vary the contract as no consideration is present.

These statements are based upon *Stilk v. Myrick*, 2 Camp. 317 and *Syros Shipping Co. S.A. v. Elaghill Trading Co.* [1980] Lloyd's Rep. 390. Reference is also made to paragraph 197 earlier in the textbook where *Stilk v. Myrick* is considered at some length. On the other hand, at paragraph 183 the editors make this proposition:

> The requirement that consideration must move from the promisee is most generally satisfied where some detriment is suffered by him: e.g. where he parts with money or goods, or renders services, in exchange for the promise. But the requirement may equally well be satisfied where the promisee confers a benefit on the promisor without in fact suffering any detriment. For example, in *De la Bere v. Pearson Ltd.* [1908] 1 K.B. 280 the defendants owned a newspaper and invited readers to apply for financial advice on the terms that the defendants should be entitled to publish the readers' letters and their own replies.

This is an accurate recital of the facts in *De la Bere v. Pearson Ltd.* [1908] 1 K.B. 280 but when the argument and judgments are read the case turned on issues other than consideration, namely remoteness of damage, etc. So the case is doubtful support for the proposition made in this paragraph.

The question must be posed: what consideration has moved from the plaintiff to support the promise to pay the extra £10,300 added to the lump sum provision? In the particular circumstances which I have outlined above, there was clearly a commercial advantage to both sides from a pragmatic point of view in reaching the agreement of 9 April.

The defendants were on risk that as a result of the bargain they had struck the plaintiff would not or indeed possibly could not comply with his existing obligations without further finance. As a result of the agreement the defendants secured their position commercially. There was, however, no obligation added to the contractual duties imposed upon the plaintiff under the original contract. Prima facie this would appear to be a classic *Stilk v. Myrick* case. It was, however, open to the plaintiff to be in deliberate breach of the contract in order to "cut his losses" commercially. In normal circumstances the suggestion that a contracting party can rely upon his own breach to establish consideration is distinctly unattractive. In many cases it obviously would be and if there was any element of duress brought upon the other contracting party under the modern development of this branch of the law the proposed breaker of the contract would not benefit. With some hesitation and comforted by the passage from the speech of Lord Hailsham of St. Marylebone L.C. in *Woodhouse A.C. Israel Cocoa Ltd. S.A. v. Nigerian Produce Marketing Co. Ltd.* [1972] A.C. 741, 757–758, to which I have referred, I consider that the modern approach to the question of consideration would be that where there were benefits derived by each party to a contract of variation even though one party did not suffer a detriment this would not be fatal to the establishing of sufficient consideration to support the agreement. If both parties benefit from an agreement it is not necessary that each also suffers a detriment. In my judgment, on the facts as found by the judge, he was entitled to reach the conclusion that consideration existed and in those circumstances I would not disturb that finding. This is sufficient to determine the appeal. The judge found as a fact that the flats were "substantially completed" and that payment was due to the plaintiff in respect of the number of flats substantially completed which left an outstanding amount due from the defendants to the plaintiff in the absence of the payment of which the plaintiff was entitled to remove from the site. For these reasons and for the reasons which have already been given by Glidewell L.J. I would dismiss this appeal.

Another interesting English case is the recent UK Supreme Court decision *MWB Business Exchange Centres Ltd v Rock Advertising Ltd.*[20]

20 *MWB Business Exchange Centres Ltd v Rock Advertising Ltd* [2018] UKSC 24.

Rock, an advertising agency, entered into a year's licence agreement with MWB to occupy serviced office premises in central London, with a monthly fee of £3,500 for the first three months, thereafter £4,433.34. After the first four months, however, Rock had only paid a small fraction of its monthly fees, and had already incurred arrears of over £12,000. Rock's managing director Mr Idehen had a telephone conversation with Ms Evans, a credit controller at MWB, in which he proposed rescheduling the remaining payments: Rock would pay less than the originally agreed amount for the first few months, thereafter it would pay more, clearing the arrears by the end of the year. This conversation formed the nub of the dispute: on the one side, Mr Idehan thought it concluded a binding oral agreement, and made an immediate payment of £3,500 accordingly, while, on the other side, Ms Evans treated it as a mere proposal in a continuing negotiation. Two days later she emailed Mr Idehan rejecting the proposal, stating that her boss, MWB's finance director was "not happy to allow you to accumulate any more debt on the account". MWB gave notice terminating the licence agreement and sued for unpaid arrears, whereupon Rock counterclaimed for damages for wrongful exclusion.

At first instance MWB's submissions were upheld: the Central London County Court found that an oral agreement had been made to vary the licence, and that the variation was supported by consideration, because it brought practical advantages to MWB, in that the prospect of being paid eventually was enhanced. Nonetheless, the variation was ineffective because it was not recorded in writing signed on behalf of both parties, as required by a contract clause prescribing formal requirements for contractual modification (no oral modification clause, NOM).

The Court of Appeal unanimously allowed Rock's appeal, confirming that the oral variation was supported by consideration, but dissenting on its validity, in the sense that the oral variation was effective despite its non-compliance with the NOM clause. For the Court of Appeal the principle of freedom of contract and autonomy means that sovereign parties are free to depart from their previously agreed NOM regime.

The Supreme Court unanimously allowed MWB's appeal. According to Lord Sumption (with whom Lady Hale, Lord Wilson and Lord Lloyd-Jones agreed) "the law should and does give effect to a contractual provision requiring specified formalities to be observed for a variation". The effect of the Court of Appeal's decision was in fact to override the parties' intentions: "They cannot validly bind themselves as to the manner in which future changes in their legal relations are to be achieved, however clearly they express their intention to do so". The perceived conceptual problem of party autonomy was a "fallacy":

> Party autonomy operates up to the point when the contract is made, but thereafter only to the extent that the contract allows. Nearly all contracts bind the parties to some course of action, and to that extent restrict their autonomy. The real offence against party autonomy is the suggestion that they cannot bind themselves as to the form of any variation, even if that is what they have agreed. (see no° [11] of the judgment).

Moreover, he convincingly rejected the Court of Appeal's elision of an intention to vary the licence agreement and an intention to depart from the NOM clause.

> [W]hat of the theory that parties who agree an oral variation in spite of a No Oral Modification clause must have intended to dispense with the clause? This does not seem to me to follow. What the parties to such a clause have agreed is not that oral variations are forbidden, but that they will be invalid. The mere fact of agreeing to an oral variation is not therefore a contravention of the clause. It is simply the situation to which the clause applies. It is not difficult to record a variation in writing, except perhaps in cases where the variation is so complex that no sensible businessman would do anything else. The natural inference from the parties' failure to observe the formal requirements of a No Oral Modification clause is not that they intended to dispense with it but that they overlooked it. If, on the other hand, they had it in mind, then they were courting invalidity with their eyes open.

The issue of consideration in this case is not faced directly by the Supreme Court. As previously observed, contracts can be varied orally, but consideration is required for any variation. As this requisite is controversial in practice, contractual drafters very often prescribe formal requirements for contract modification, precisely with the NOM clause. In this case, the Supreme Court focussed its attention on making clear that these clauses are totally valid, but concerning the issue of consideration the Court thought it "unnecessary" and "undesirable" to consider whether the oral variation was supported by consideration. According to Lord Sumption "the issue is a difficult one". So even after this case the issue concerning consideration in the field of variation of contracts remains still uncertain. As one author points out, let us consider that the parties in this cause had complied with the NOM clause, but again MWB had purported to renege on the variation immediately, before Rock had taken any action in reliance. Should Rock still have to prove consideration or would such compliance take the variation outside the requirement of consideration altogether? Alternatively, would going through the formal steps in the NOM clause be treated as providing consideration? These questions remain unanswered.[21]

3.4.2 The civil law approach

In contrast, in the civil law countries contract variation seems not to be problematic. Some European civil codes provide that in order to modify a contract the mutual agreement of the parties is needed (see for instance Art. 1193 French civil code) and the majority of European civil codes do not expressly mention the modification of contracts, so the same rules for the conclusion of contracts apply.

At an international level it is worth mentioning Article 29 of CISG: "A contract may be modified or terminated by the mere agreement of the parties". By specifying "mere agreement", this provision makes clear that in order to modify the contract nothing else is necessary apart from the mutual consent of the parties.

It is also interesting to note that the continental codes usually provide that it is possible for the creditor to release the debt, totally or partially. For example, in Italian law Art. 1236 admits explicitly the voluntary discharge of a duty, even unilaterally and without any formality, provided that the debtor

21 J. O'Sullivan, 'Party-Agreed Formalities for Contractual Variation – A Rock of Sense in the Supreme Court?' *LQR* 2019, 1.

does not refuse. In this way it is always possible for the creditor to discharge the debtor to perform its obligation, and this shows that in the civil law tradition there are several options for modifying a contract with no other requisite than the consent of the parties. Modern civil law does not provide for any requirement of sufficient cause or form with reference to the release and promise not to sue. That is, the form of donation is not necessary even when they are made with an intent of liberality.[22]

Similarly, according to Article 5.1.9 of the UNIDROIT Principles "An obligee may release its right by agreement with the obligor. An offer to release a right gratuitously shall be deemed accepted if the obligor does not reject the offer without delay after having become aware of it".[23]

3.5 The problem of firm offers

A second issue concerns firm offers: if an offer expressly contains a period within which it has to be accepted, is the offeror obliged to keep the offer open during that period?

The case *Dickinson v Dodds*[24] illustrates the situation in English law: no binding obligation can arise without consideration.

According to the Court of Appeal an offer to sell property may be withdrawn before acceptance without any formal notice to the person to whom the offer is made. It is sufficient if that person has actual knowledge that the person who made the offer has done some act inconsistent with the continuance of the offer, such as selling the property to a third person.

Facts. On Wednesday, 10 June 1874, the defendant John Dodds signed and delivered to the plaintiff, George Dickinson, a memorandum of which the material part was as follows:

> I hereby agree to sell to Mr. George Dickinson the whole of the dwelling-houses, garden ground, stabling, and outbuildings thereto

22 G. Gorla, *I problemi fondamentali del contratto* etc., cit., p. 237 ff. shows that the validity of the voluntary discharge and of the modifying pacts cannot be deemed an application of an alleged principle of validity of bare pacts, because they are typical pacts, binding for special reasons.

23 It is interesting to consider the Italian case Cass. civ., sec. III, 2 March 2012, no. 3245 according to which a contract can be terminated implying a mutual will to terminate by the conduct of the parties, unless a specific form is necessary.

24 *Dickinson v Dodds*, [1876] 2 ChD 463, CA.

> belonging, situate at Croft, belonging to me, for the sum of £800. As witness my hand this tenth day of June, 1874. £800. [Signed] John Dodds [...] P.S. — This offer to be left over until Friday, 9 o'clock, A.M. J. D. [the twelfth], 12th June, 1874. [[Signed] J. Dodds].

The bill alleged that Dodds understood and intended that the plaintiff should have until Friday 9 A.M. within which to determine whether he would or would not purchase, and that he should absolutely have until that time the refusal of the property at the price of £800, and that the plaintiff in fact determined to accept the offer on the morning of Thursday, 11 June, but did not at once signify his acceptance to Dodds, believing that he had the power to accept it until 9 A.M. on the Friday.

In the afternoon of the Thursday, the plaintiff was informed by a Mr. Berry that Dodds had been offering or agreeing to sell the property to Thomas Allan, the other defendant. Thereupon the plaintiff, at about half-past seven in the evening, went to the house of Mrs. Burgess, Dodds' mother-in-law, where he was then staying, and left with her a formal acceptance in writing of the offer to sell the property. According to the evidence of Mrs. Burgess this document never in fact reached Dodds, she having forgotten to give it to him.

On the following (Friday) morning, at about seven o'clock, Berry, who was acting as agent for Dickinson, found Dodds at Darlington railway station, and handed him a duplicate of the acceptance by Dickinson, and explained to Dodds its purport. He replied that it was too late, as he had sold the property. A few minutes later Dickinson himself found Dodds entering a railway carriage, and handed him another duplicate of the notice of acceptance, but Dodds declined to receive it, saying, "You are too late. I have sold the property".

It appeared that on the day before, Thursday, 11 June, Dodds had signed a formal contract for the sale of the property to the defendant Allan for £800, and had received from him a deposit of £40.

The bill in this suit stated that the defendant Dodds might be decreed specifically to perform the contract of the 10 June 1874; that he might be restrained from conveying the property to Allan; that Allan might be restrained from taking any such conveyance; that, if any such conveyance had been or should be made, Allan might be declared a trustee of the property for, and might be directed to convey the property to, the plaintiff; and for damages.

The most interesting judgment is the one given by James, L.J. The parts in italics emphasize some relevant parts of the Judge's opinion.

James L.J.

The document, though beginning "I hereby agree to sell," was nothing but an offer, and was only intended to be an offer, for the Plaintiff himself tells us that he required time to consider whether he would enter into an agreement or not. Unless both parties had then agreed there was no concluded agreement then made; it was in effect and substance only an offer to sell. The Plaintiff, being minded not to complete the bargain at that time, added this memorandum—"This offer to be left over until Friday, 9 o'clock A.M., 12th June, 1874." That shews it was only an offer. *There was no consideration given for the undertaking or promise,* to whatever extent it may be considered binding, to keep the property unsold until 9 o'clock on Friday morning; but apparently Dickinson was of opinion, and probably Dodds was of the same opinion, that he (Dodds) was bound by that promise, and could not in any way withdraw from it, or retract it, until 9 o'clock on Friday morning, and this probably explains a good deal of what afterwards took place. But *it is clear settled law, on one of the clearest principles of law, that this promise, being a mere nudum pactum, was not binding, and that at any moment before a complete acceptance* by Dickinson of the offer, Dodds was as free as Dickinson himself. Well, that being the state of things, it is said that the only mode in which Dodds could assert that freedom was by actually and distinctly saying to Dickinson, "Now I withdraw my offer." It appears to me that there is neither principle nor authority for the proposition that there must be an express and actual withdrawal of the offer, or what is called a retractation. *It must, to constitute a contract, appear that the two minds were at one,* at the same moment of time, that is, that there was an offer continuing up to the time of the acceptance. If there was not such a continuing offer, then the acceptance comes to nothing. Of course it may well be that the one man is bound in some way or other to let the other man

> know that his mind with regard to the offer has been changed; but in this case, beyond all question, the Plaintiff knew that Dodds was no longer minded to sell the property to him as plainly and clearly as if Dodds had told him in so many words, "I withdraw the offer." This is evident from the Plaintiff's own statements in the bill.
>
> The Plaintiff says in effect that, having heard and knowing that Dodds was no longer minded to sell to him, and that he was selling or had sold to some one else, thinking that he could not in point of law withdraw his offer, meaning to fix him to it, and endeavouring to bind him," "I went to the house where he was lodging, and saw his mother-in-law, and left with her an acceptance of the offer, knowing all the while that he had entirely changed his mind. I got an agent to watch for him at 7 o'clock the next morning, and I went to the train just before 9 o'clock, in order that I might catch him and give him my notice of acceptance just before 9 o'clock, and when that occurred he told my agent, and he told me, you are too late, and he then threw back the paper." It is to my mind quite clear that before there was any attempt at acceptance by the Plaintiff, he was perfectly well aware that Dodds had changed his mind, and that he had in fact agreed to sell the property to Allan. It is impossible, therefore, to say there was ever that existence of the same mind between the two parties which is essential in point of law to the making of an agreement. I am of opinion, therefore, that the Plaintiff has failed to prove that there was any binding contract between Dodds and himself.

In short, the Court of appeal concluded that the document amounted only to an offer, which might be withdrawn at any time before acceptance, and that a sale to a third person which came to the knowledge of the person to whom the offer was made was an effectual withdrawal of the offer.

The strict approach to firm offers adopted by English law is more nuanced in the US. It suffices to notice that § 2:205 of the Restatement (Second) of

Contracts provides that a firm offer cannot be revoked for lack of consideration if it comes from a merchant, it is in writing and the period does not exceed three months.

Moving to the civil law, the traditional view in French law is well expressed in a case decided by the Court of Cassation.[25]

In a letter of 11 August 1954 Mr. Isler informed Mr. Chastan that he was willing to sell a chalet owned by him. Mr. Chastan wrote to Isler announcing a visit to the chalet on the 15 or 16 August and after the visit he notified Isler by telegram that he accepted the offer. On 17 August 1954 he also confirmed his acceptance by letter, stating that he was willing to pay the purchase price at the moment of signing the deed. On 6 September 1954 Chastan served formal notice on Isler requiring him to accept the purchase price and to hand over the keys, but Isler did not comply with this. Chastan brought legal proceedings. Isler alleged that on 16 August 1954 he had already sold the chalet to a third person, who intervened in the proceedings stating that the sale of the chalet took place at the beginning of August and was formalized by deed on 14 August 1954. The Court concluded in favour of the buyer Chastan.

> Whereas whilst an offer may in principle be revoked at any time prior to its acceptance, that is not the position where the person making it has expressly or impliedly undertaken not to revoke it before a certain date;
>
> Whereas in the present case the contested judgment, having acknowledged that the letter of 11 August 1954 constituted "merely an offer to sell" which could "in principle be revoked at any time prior to being accepted" goes on to state: "however Isler, knowing from a letter from Chastan dated 9 August that the latter was proposing to visit the chalet on 15 or 16 August, and having authorised him to do so in his reply of 11 August, tacitly undertook to keep his offer open during the period thus envisaged, that is to say, until after the proposed visit had taken

25 Cass. Civ., 17 December 1958. The original text is published in Rec. Dalloz, 1959, 1, p. 33. For this translation: © H. Beale, B. Fauvarque-Cosson, J. Rutgers, S. Vogenauer, *Cases, Materials and Text on Contract Law*, 3rd ed., London, Hart Publishing, 2019, p. 198, an imprint of Bloomsbury Publishing plc.

> place" and that Isler could not therefore have withdrawn from the transaction on 14 August without incurring liability [...]
>
> Whereas it follows that the appealed judgment did not infringe the legislation referred to in the appellant's pleadings and is well grounded in law.

In short, the revocation of offer is valid, but the offeror is liable to pay damages for the loss the offeree has suffered from the untimely revocation.

With the 2016 reform of the law of obligations and contracts, the new Article 1116 now provides that the offer cannot be revoked before the expiration of the promised period; if it is revoked before, the offeror breaching his promise is liable in tort (but the *lucrum cessant* is excluded).

German law follows a different approach. According to § 148 BGB "If the offeror has determined a period of time for the acceptance of an offer, the acceptance may only take place within this period". This means that the revocation has no effect, the offeree can still accept and thus conclude the contract.

Italian law takes the same position. Art. 1329 of the Italian civil code provides that if the offeror binds himself to keep the offer for a certain period of time, its revocation before the time limit has no effect.

The UNIDROIT Principles follow the German/Italian solution. According to Art. 2.1.4, an offer is irrevocable if it indicates that it is irrevocable or if it was reasonable for the offeree to rely on the offer as being irrevocable and the offeree has acted in reliance on it. The same is stated in the CISG where Art. 16 provides that an offer cannot be revoked

> if it indicates, whether by stating a fixed time for acceptance or otherwise, that it is irrevocable or if it was reasonable for the offeree to rely on the offer as being irrevocable and the offeree has acted in reliance on the offer.

4 The formation of contracts

The general rule is that the formation of contract takes place through an offer accepted by the other party. The meeting of the two constitutes the agreement. Put in this way, the rule seems very simple. However, significant differences in the mechanism of formation of contract derive from the different conceptions of contract highlighted in the previous chapter. Very briefly, in the civil law tradition the scheme of offer and acceptance is seen as the way through which the parties express their will. Consequently, acceptance is the manifestation of the intention to agree to the offer, giving rise to the conclusion of contract. From the common law perspective, the idea that reliance of the other party is relevant in order to create a binding obligation leads to shaping a clear distinction between an invitation to treat and an offer. Moreover, as acceptance essentially coincides with the consideration for the enforceability of the promise, an 'objective' approach is adopted in order to ascertain an offer and an acceptance.

4.1 Offer and invitation to treat: a controversial distinction

The offer/acceptance scheme is criticized for many reasons. The most relevant one is that it is purported to be generally applicable, whereas contracts are made in different ways: in writing, orally, after long negotiations or instantaneously, by conduct of the parties, etc. It is almost impossible to frame rules that can be applied across such a broad spectrum. We will consider a critical situation which is useful to show a relevant difference between the civil law and the common law approaches. Does the display of goods amount

DOI: 10.4324/9781003251606-4

to an offer? The answer followed in most civil law countries is affirmative if the necessary elements to form a contract (essentially the price) are clear. Instead, English law clearly distinguishes between offer and invitation to treat.

The case *Fisher v Bell*, decided by the High Court in 1960, is very interesting in this respect.[1]

On 14 December 1959, an information was preferred by Chief Inspector George Fisher, of the Bristol Constabulary, against James Charles Bell, the defendant, alleging that the defendant, on 26 October 1959, at his premises in The Arcade, Broadmead, Bristol, unlawfully offered for sale a knife which had a blade which opened automatically by hand pressure applied to a device attached to the handle of the knife (commonly referred to as a 'flick knife') contrary to section 1 of the Restriction of Offensive Weapons Act, 1959.

The justices heard the information on 3 February 1960, and found the following facts: the defendant was the occupier of a shop and premises situated at 15–16, The Arcade, Broadmead, at which premises he carried on the business of a retail shopkeeper, trading under the name of Bell's Music Shop. At 3.15 p.m. on 26 October 1959, Police Constable John Kingston saw displayed in the window of the shop amongst other articles a knife, behind which was a ticket upon which the words 'Ejector knife – 4s.' were printed. The words referred to the knife in question. The police constable entered the shop, saw the defendant and said he had reason to believe it was a flick knife displayed in the shop window. He asked if he might examine the knife. The defendant removed the knife from the window and said he had had other policemen in there about the knives. The constable examined the knife and pursuant to the invitation of the defendant took it away from the premises for examination by a superintendent of police. Later the same day he returned to the defendant's premises and informed him that in his opinion the knife was a flick knife. The defendant said, "Why do manufacturers still bring them round for us to sell?" The constable informed the defendant that he would be reported for offering for sale a flick knife and the defendant replied, "Fair enough".

It was contended by the prosecutor that the defendant by his actions in displaying the knife in the window with the ticket behind it and referring to it, such actions being carried out with the object of attracting the attention of a buyer of such knife and selling the same to such buyer, had on the day

1 *Fisher v Bell* [1960] 3 WLR 919.

in question offered the knife for sale within the meaning of the Restriction of Offensive Weapons Act, 1959.

It was contended by the defendant that on the facts he at no time offered the knife for sale within the meaning of the Act.

The justices were of the opinion that in the absence of a definition in the Act of 1959, the words 'offer for sale' ought to be construed as they were in the law of contract, so that, in this instance, the defendant's action was but an invitation to treat, and not an offer which needed but a customer's acceptance to make a binding contract of sale. They accordingly dismissed the information. The prosecutor appealed.

Lord Parker

The sole question is whether the exhibition of that knife in the window with the ticket constituted an offer for sale within the statute. I confess that I think most lay people and, indeed, I myself when I first read the papers, would be inclined to the view that to say that if a knife was displayed in a window like that with a price attached to it was not offering it for sale was just nonsense. In ordinary language it is there inviting people to buy it, and it is for sale; but any statute must of course be looked at in the light of the general law of the country. Parliament in its wisdom in passing an Act must be taken to know the general law. It is perfectly clear that according to the ordinary law of contract the display of an article with a price on it in a shop window is merely an invitation to treat. It is in no sense an offer for sale the acceptance of which constitutes a contract. That is clearly the general law of the country. Not only is that so, but it is to be observed that in many statutes and orders which prohibit selling and offering for sale of goods it is very common when it is so desired to insert the words "offering or exposing for sale," "exposing for sale" being clearly words which would cover the display of goods in a shop window. Not only that, but it appears that under several statutes—we have been referred in particular to the Prices of Goods Act, 1939, and the Goods and

Services (Price Control) Act, 1941—Parliament, when it desires to enlarge the ordinary meaning of those words, includes a definition section enlarging the ordinary meaning of "offer for sale" to cover other matters including, be it observed, exposure of goods for sale with the price attached.

In those circumstances I am driven to the conclusion, though I confess reluctantly, that no offence was here committed. At first sight it sounds absurd that knives of this sort cannot be manufactured, sold, hired, lent, or given, but apparently they can be displayed in shop windows; but even if this—and I am by no means saying it is—is a casus omissus it is not for this court to supply the omission. I am mindful of the strong words of Lord Simonds in *Magor and St. Mellons Rural District Council v. Newport Corporation*. In that case one of the Lords Justices in the Court of Appeal had, in effect, said that the court having discovered the supposed intention of Parliament must proceed to fill in the gaps—what the Legislature has not written the court must write—and in answer to that contention Lord Simonds in his speech said:

> It appears to me to be a naked usurpation of the legislative function under the thin disguise of interpretation.

Approaching this matter apart from authority, I find it quite impossible to say that an exhibition of goods in a shop window is itself an offer for sale. We were, however, referred to several cases, one of which is *Keating v. Horwood* a decision of this court. There, a baker's van was being driven on its rounds. There was bread in it that had been ordered and bread in it that was for sale, and it was found that that bread was under weight contrary to the Sale of Food Order, 1921. That order was an order of the sort to which I have referred already which prohibited the offering or exposing for sale. In giving his judgment, Lord Hewart C.J. said this: "The question is whether on the facts there were, (1) an offering, and (2) an exposure, for sale. In my opinion, there were both." Avory J. said: "I agree and have nothing to add". Shearman J., however, said:

> I am of the same opinion. I am quite clear that this bread was exposed for sale, but have some doubt whether it can be said to have been offered for sale until a particular loaf was tendered to a particular customer.

There are three matters to observe on that case. The first is that the order plainly contained the words "expose for sale," and on any view there was an exposing for sale. Therefore the question whether there was an offer for sale was unnecessary for decision. Secondly, the principles of general contract law were never referred to, and thirdly, albeit all part of the second ground, the respondent was not represented and there was in fact no argument. I cannot take that as an authority for the proposition that the display here in a shop window was an offer for sale.

The other case to which I should refer is *Wiles v. Maddison*. I find it unnecessary to go through the facts of that case, which was a very different case and where all that was proved was an intention to commit an offence the next day, but in the course of his judgment Viscount Caldecote C.J. said:

> A person might, for instance, be convicted of making an offer of an article of food at too high a price by putting it in his shop window to be sold at an excessive price, although there would be no evidence of anybody having passed the shop window or having seen the offer or the exposure of the article for sale at that price.

Again, be it observed, that was a case where under the Meat (Maximum Retail Prices) Order, 1940, the words were "No person shall sell or offer or expose for sale or buy or offer to buy".

Although the Lord Chief Justice does refer to the making of an offer by putting it in the shop window, before the sentence is closed he has in fact turned the phrase to one of exposing the article. I cannot get any assistance in favour of the prosecutor from that passage. Accordingly, I have come to the conclusion in this case that the justices were right, and this appeal must be dismissed.

Another critical point is related to the way adopted in order to settle whether an offer has been made by one party and accepted by the other. From a general point of view, the 'intention of the parties' plays a crucial role in the civil law countries. It is a clear consequence of the will theory, according to which no contract can arise if the parties did not intend to be bound. Their subjective intention is to be ascertained. In contrast, the English approach is that the words as objectively understandable by a reasonable person are relevant, but not the parties' subjective intentions.

The English case *Gibson v Manchester City Council* clearly illustrates the English approach.[2] Emphasis is added in order to attract attention on the Judge's way of reasoning.

Lord Diplock

This is an action for specific performance of what is claimed to be a contract for the sale of land. The only question in the appeal is of a kind with which the courts are very familiar. It is whether in the correspondence between the parties there can be found a legally enforceable contract for the sale by the Manchester Corporation to Mr. Gibson of the dwelling-house of which he was the occupying tenant at the relevant time in 1971. That question is one that, in my view, can be answered by applying to the particular documents relied upon by Mr. Gibson as constituting the contract, *well-settled, indeed elementary, principles*

2 [1979] WLR 294.

of English law. This being so, it is not the sort of case in which leave would have been likely to be granted to appeal to your Lordships' House, but for the fact that it is a test case.

The two documents principally relied upon by Mr. Gibson were in standard forms used by the corporation in dealing with applications from tenants of council houses to purchase the freehold of their homes under a scheme that had been adopted by the council during a period when it was under Conservative Party control. Political control passed to the Labour Party as a result of the local government elections held in May 1971. The scheme was then abandoned. It was decided that no more council houses should be sold to any tenant with whom a legally binding contract of sale had not already been concluded. At the date of this decision there was a considerable number of tenants, running into hundreds, whose applications to purchase the houses which they occupied had reached substantially the same stage as that of Mr. Gibson. The two documents in the same standard form as those on which he principally relies had passed between each one of them and the corporation. So their rights too are likely to depend upon the result of this appeal.

My Lords, the contract of which specific performance is sought to be enforced is a contract for the sale of land. It is thus subject to the requirements as to writing laid down in section 40 of the Law of Property Act 1925; but nothing turns on this since the only contract that is alleged is one made by letters and accompanying documents passing between the parties. The outcome of this appeal depends upon their true construction.

In the Manchester County Court where the action started, the case was pleaded in the conventional way. The particulars of claim alleged an offer in writing by the corporation to sell the freehold interest in the house to Mr. Gibson at a price of £2,180 and an acceptance in writing of that offer by Mr. Gibson. The judge (Judge Bailey) followed the same conventional approach to the question that fell to be decided. He looked to see whether there was an offer of sale and an acceptance. He held that, upon their true construction, the documents relied upon as such in the particulars of claim did amount to an offer and an acceptance respectively and so constituted a legally enforceable contract. He ordered specific performance of an open contract for the sale to Mr. Gibson of the freehold interest in the house at the price of £2,180.

The corporation's appeal against this judgment was dismissed by a majority of the Court of Appeal (Lord Denning M.R. and Ormrod L.J.); Geoffrey Lane L.J. dissented. Lord Denning M.R. rejected what I have described as the conventional approach of looking to see whether upon the true construction of the documents relied upon there can be discerned an offer and acceptance. One ought, he said, to "look at the correspondence" as a whole and at the conduct of the parties and see therefrom whether "the parties have come to an agreement on everything that was material".

This approach, which in referring to the conduct of the parties where there is no allegation of part performance appears to me to overlook the provisions of section 40 of the Law of Property Act 1925, led him however to the conclusion that there should be imported into the agreement to be specifically performed additional conditions, against use except as a private dwelling-house and against advertising and a restriction not to sell or lease the property for five years. These are conditions which would not be implied by law in an open contract for the sale of land. The reason for so varying the county court judge's order was that clauses in these terms were included in the standard form of "Agreement for Sale of a Council House" which, as appears from the earlier case of *Storer v. Manchester City Council* [1974]1 WLR 1403, was entered into by the Corporation and council tenants whose applications to purchase the freehold of their council house reached the stage at which contracts were exchanged. There was, however, no reference to this standard form of agreement in any of the documents said to constitute the contract relied on in the instant case, nor was there any evidence that Mr. Gibson had knowledge of its terms at or before the time that the alleged contract was concluded.

Lord Justice Ormrod, who agreed with the Master of the Rolls, adopted a similar approach but he did also deal briefly with the construction of the document relied upon by Mr. Gibson as an unconditional offer of sale by the corporation. On this he came to the same conclusion as the county court judge.

Lord Justice Geoffrey Lane in a dissenting judgment, which for my part I find convincing, adopted the conventional approach. He found that upon the true construction of the documents relied upon as constituting the contract, there never was an offer by the corporation acceptance of which by Mr. Gibson was capable in law of constituting a legally enforceable contract. It was but a step in the negotiations for a contract which, owing to the change in the political complexion of the council, never reached fruition.

My Lords, there may be certain types of contract, though I think they are exceptional, which do not fit easily into the normal analysis of a contract as being constituted by offer and acceptance; but a contract alleged to have been made by an exchange of correspondence between the parties in which the successive communications other than the first are in reply to one another, is not one of these. *I can see no reason in the instant case for departing from the conventional approach of looking at the handful of documents relied upon as constituting the contract sued upon and seeing whether upon their true construction there is to be found in them a contractual offer by the corporation to sell the house to Mr. Gibson and an acceptance of that offer by Mr. Gibson.* I venture to think that it was by departing from this conventional approach that the majority of the Court of Appeal was led into error.

The genesis of the relevant negotiations in the instant case is a form filled in by Mr. Gibson on 28 November 1970 inquiring what would be the price of buying his council house at 174 Charlestown Road, Blackley, and expressing his interest in obtaining a mortgage from the corporation. The form was a detachable part of a brochure which had been circulated by the corporation to tenants who had previously expressed an interest in buying their houses. It contained details of a new scheme for selling council houses that had been recently adopted by the council. The scheme provided for a sale at market value less a discount dependent on the length of time the purchaser had been a council tenant. This, in the case of Mr. Gibson would have amounted to 20%. The scheme also provided for the provision by the corporation of advances upon mortgage which might amount to as much as the whole of the purchase price.

As a result of that inquiry Mr. Gibson's house was inspected by the corporation's valuer and on 10 February 1971 the letter which is relied upon by Mr. Gibson as the offer by the corporation to sell the house to him was sent from the City Treasurer's Department. It was in the following terms:

> Dear Sir,
> Purchase of Council House
> Your Reference Number 82463 03
> "I refer to your request for details of the cost of buying your Council" house. The Corporation may be prepared to sell the house to you at "the purchase price of £2,725 less 20% =£2,180 (freehold).
> "Maximum mortgage the Corporation may grant : £2,177 repayable" over 20 years
> "Annual fire insurance premium : £2.45"

> Monthly Repayment charge calculated by"(i) flat rate repayment method: £19.02 [...].
> If you wish to pay off some of the purchase price at the start and therefore require a mortgage for less than the amount quoted above, the monthly instalment will change; in these circumstances, I will "supply new figures on request The above repayment figures apply so long as the interest rate charged on home loans is 8½%. The interest rate will be subject to variation by the Corporation after giving not less than three months' written notice, and if it changes, there will be an adjustment to the monthly instalment payable. This letter should not be regarded as firm offer of a mortgage.
> *If you would like to make formal application to buy your Council house, please complete the enclosed application form and return it to me as soon as possible.* Yours faithfully (Sgd) H. R. PAGECITY TREASURER

My Lords, the words I have italicised seem to me, as they seemed to Geoffrey Lane L.J., to make it quite impossible to construe this letter as a contractual offer capable of being converted into a legally enforceable open contract for the sale of land by Mr. Gibson's written acceptance of it. *The words "may be prepared to sell" are fatal to this; so is the invitation, not, be it noted, to accept the offer, but "to make formal application to buy" upon the enclosed application form.* It is, to quote Geoffrey Lane L.J., a letter setting out the financial terms on which it may be the council will be prepared to consider a sale and purchase in due course.

Both Ormrod L.J. and the county court judge in reaching the conclusion that this letter was a firm offer to sell the freehold interest in the house for £2,180, attached importance to the fact that the second paragraph, dealing with the financial details of the mortgage of which Mr. Gibson had asked for particulars, stated expressly, "This letter should not be regarded as a firm offer of a mortgage". The necessary implication from this, it is suggested, is that the first paragraph of the letter is to be regarded as a firm offer to sell despite the fact that this is plainly inconsistent with the express language of that paragraph. My Lords, with great respect, this surely must be fallacious. If the final sentence had been omitted the wording of the second paragraph, unlike that of the first, with its use of the indicative mood in such expressions as "the interest rate will change", might have been understood by council tenants to whom it was addressed as indicating a firm offer of a mortgage of the amount and on the terms for repayment stated if the council were prepared to sell the house at the stated price.

But whether or not this be the explanation of the presence of the last sentence in paragraph 2, it cannot possibly affect the plain meaning of the words used in paragraph 1.

Mr. Gibson did fill in the application form enclosed with this letter. It was in three sections; section A headed "Application to buy a council house". Section B "Application for a loan to buy a council house" and section C "Certificate to be completed by all applicants." He left blank the space for the purchase price in section A and sent the form to the corporation on 5 March 1971 with a covering letter in which he requested the corporation either to undertake at their own expense to carry out repairs to the tarmac path forming part of the premises or to make a deduction from the purchase price to cover the cost of repairs. The letter also intimated that Mr. Gibson would like to make a down payment of £500 towards the purchase price instead of borrowing the whole amount on mortgage. In reply to the request made in this letter the corporation, by letter of 12 March 1971, said that the condition of the property had been taken into consideration in fixing the purchase price and that repairs to the tarmac by the corporation could not be authorised at this stage. This letter was acknowledged by Mr. Gibson by his letter to the corporation of 18 March 1971 in which he asked the corporation to "carry on with the purchase as per my application already in your possession."

My Lords, the application form and letter of 18 March 1971 were relied on by Mr. Gibson as an unconditional acceptance of the corporation's offer to sell the house; but this cannot be so unless there was a contractual offer by the corporation available for acceptance, and, for the reason already given I am of opinion that there was none. It is unnecessary to consider whether the application form and Mr. Gibson's letters of 3 and 18 March 1971 are capable of amounting to a contractual offer by him to purchase the freehold interest in the house at a price of £2,180 on the terms of an open contract, for there is no suggestion that, even if it were, it was ever accepted by the corporation. Nor would it ever have been even if there had been no change in the political control of the council, as the policy of the corporation before the change required the incorporation in all agreements for sale of council houses to tenants of the conditions referred by the Master of the Rolls in his judgment and other conditions inconsistent with an open contract.

I therefore feel compelled to allow the appeal. One can sympathise with Mr. Gibson's disappointment on finding that his expectations that he would be able to buy his council house at 20 per cent below its market value in the autumn of 1970 cannot be realised. Whether one thinks this makes it a hard case perhaps depends upon the political views that one holds about council housing policy. But hard cases offer a strong temptation to let them have their proverbial consequences. It is a temptation that the judicial mind must be vigilant to resist.

4.2 When is a contract concluded?

The general rule is that an acceptance must be communicated in order to be effective. However sometimes an offer invites acceptance by conduct and in this case it suffices that the offeree has done what was requested by the offeror, such as shipping the goods.

The international legal rules reflect the main legal principles in this respect.

PECL

Art. 2:205

(1) If an acceptance has been dispatched by the offeree the contract is concluded when the acceptance reaches the offeror.
(2) In case of acceptance by conduct, the contract is concluded when notice of the conduct reaches the offeror.
(3) If by virtue of the offer, of practices which the parties have established between themselves, or of a usage, the offeree may accept the offer by performing an act without notice to the offeror, the contract is concluded when the performance of the act begins.

UNIDROIT PICC

Art. 2.6 (2)

An acceptance of an offer becomes effective when the indication of assent reaches the offeror.

Art. 2.4 (1)

Until a contract is concluded an offer may be revoked if the revocation reaches the offeree before it has dispatched an acceptance.

Art. 2.10

An acceptance may be withdrawn if the withdrawal reaches the offeror before or at the same time as the acceptance would have become effective.

CISG

Art. 23

A contract is concluded at the moment when an acceptance of an offer becomes effective in accordance with the provisions of this Convention.

Art. 16

Until a contract is concluded an offer may be revoked if the revocation reaches the offeree before he has dispatched an acceptance.

The texts reproduced above are a good introduction for considering the issue concerning non-instantaneous communications. Indeed, there are no particular problems if the parties conclude the contract in each other's presence or using an instantaneous communication. The situation is different when a contract is concluded through a different means of communication, such as the post.

Traditionally this issue has always been a difficult one because of the different rules adopted in the common law legal systems, in contrast with the ones followed in civil law. These differences persist, but they are now not so problematic because of the diffusion of instantaneous means of communication, enabling the parties to reach a simultaneous exchange of offer and acceptance even if the parties are at a great distance from each other. However, it is useful to consider the two competing theories.

In short, English law follows the expedition or dispatch theory: the contract is concluded when the offer is posted, so when it is sent. This is the 'mail box rule' fixed since the leading case *Adam v Lindsell* at the beginning of the

19th century.[3] The postal rule applies for purposes of determining whether an offer can still be revoked and whether a contract has been concluded if the acceptance is lost or delayed in the post. The function performed by the postal rule is to limit the offeror's power to revoke, because once the letter containing the acceptance is posted, the contract is concluded and so the offeror can no longer revoke the offer. Moreover, there will be a contract even if the letter never arrives.

The implications of the mail box rule are well described in *Byrne v Van Tienhoven*, concerning the revocation of offer.[4]

Lindley, J.

This was an action for the recovery of damages for the non-delivery by the defendants to the plaintiffs of 1000 boxes of tinplates, pursuant to an alleged contract, which I will refer to presently. The action was tried at Cardiff before myself without a jury; and it was agreed at the trial that in the event of the plaintiffs being entitled to damages they should be 375l.

The defendants carried on business at Cardiff and the plaintiffs at New York, and it takes ten or eleven days for a letter posted at either place to reach the other. The alleged contract consists of a letter written by the defendants to the plaintiffs on the 1st of October, 1879, and received by them on the 11th, and accepted by telegram and letter sent to the defendants on the 11th and 15th of October respectively. These letters and telegram were as follows:—[The learned judge read the letter of the 1st of October, 1879, from the defendants to the plaintiffs. It contained a reference to the price of tinplates branded "Hensol," and the "offer of 1000 boxes of this brand 14 × 20 at 15s. 6d. per box f. o. b. here with 1 per cent. for our commission; terms, four months' bankers' acceptance on London or Liverpool against shipping documents,

3 [1818] 1 B & Ald. 681, 106 ER 250.

4 *Byrne v Van Tienhoven* Common Pleas Division 1880. Emphasis is added in order to attract attention on the most relevant *dicta*.

but subject to your cable on or before the 15th inst. here." The answer was a telegram from the plaintiffs to the defendants sent on the 11th of October, 1879: "Accept thousand Hensols." On the 15th of October, 1879, the plaintiffs wrote to the defendants: "We have to thank you for your valued letter under date 1st inst., which we had on Saturday P.M., and immediately cabled acceptance of the 1000 boxes "Hensol," 1c. 14/20 as offered. Against this transaction we have pleasure in handing you herewith the Canadian Bank of Commerce letter of credit No. 78, October 13th, on Messrs. A. R. McMaster & Brothers, London, for 1000l. [...] Will thank you to ship the 1000 'Hensols' without delay."] These letters and telegram would, if they stood alone, plainly constitute a contract binding on both parties. [...] The defendants, however, raise two other defences to the action which remain to be considered. First, they say that the offer made by their letter of the 1st of October was revoked by them before it had been accepted by the plaintiffs by their telegram of the 11th or letter of the 15th. The facts as to these are as follows: On the 8th of October the defendants wrote and sent by post to the plaintiffs a letter withdrawing their offer of the 1st. The material part of this letter was as follows: "Confirming our respects of the 1st inst. we hasten to inform you that there having been a regular panic in the tinplate market during the last few days, which has caused prices to run up about twenty-five per cent. we are reluctantly compelled to withdraw any offer we have made to our constituents, and must therefore also consider our offer to you for 1000 boxes 'Hensols' at 17s. 6d. to be cancelled from this date." This letter of the 8th of October reached the plaintiffs on the 20th of October. On the same day the plaintiffs telegraphed to the defendants demanding shipment, and sent them a letter insisting on completion of the contract. [...]

There is no doubt that an offer can be withdrawn before it is accepted, and it is immaterial whether the offer is expressed to be open for acceptance for a given time or not: *Routledge v. Grant.*[1] For the decision of the present case, however, *it is necessary to consider two other questions, viz.: 1. Whether a withdrawal of an offer has any effect until it is communicated to the person to whom the offer has been sent? 2. Whether posting a letter of withdrawal is a communication to the person to whom the letter is sent?*

It is curious that neither of these questions appears to have been actually decided in this country. As regards the first question, *I am aware that Pothier and some other writers of celebrity are of opinion that there can be no contract if an offer is withdrawn before it is accepted,* although the withdrawal is not communicated to the person to whom the offer has been made. The reason for this opinion is that there is not in fact any such consent by both parties as is essential to constitute a contract between them. Against this view, however, it has been urged that a state of mind not notified cannot be regarded in dealings between man and man; and that an uncommunicated revocation is for all practical purposes and in point of law no revocation at all. This is the view taken in the United States: see *Tayloe v. Merchants Fire Insurance Co.[2]* cited in Benjamin on Sales, pp. 56–58, and it is adopted by Mr. Benjamin. The same view is taken by Mr. Pollock in his excellent work on Principles of Contract, ed. ii., p. 10, and by Mr. Leake in his Digest of the Law of Contracts, p. 43. *This view, moreover, appears to me much more in accordance with the general principles of English law than the view maintained by Pothier.*

I pass, therefore, to the next question, viz., *whether posting the letter of revocation was a sufficient communication of it to the plaintiff. The offer was posted on the 1st of October, the withdrawal was posted on the 8th, and did not reach the plaintiff until after he had posted his letter of the 11th, accepting the offer. It may be taken as now settled that where an offer is made and accepted by letters sent through the post, the contract is completed the moment the letter accepting the offer is posted: Harris' Case[3]; Dunlop v. Higgins[4],* even although it never reaches its destination. When, however, these authorities are looked at, it will be seen that they are based upon the principle that the writer of the offer has expressly or impliedly assented to treat an answer to him by a letter duly posted as a sufficient acceptance and notification to himself, or, in other words, he has made the post office his agent to receive the acceptance and notification of it. But this principle appears to me to be inapplicable to the case of the withdrawal of an offer. In this particular case I can find no evidence of any authority in fact given by the plaintiffs to the defendants to notify a withdrawal of their offer by merely posting a letter; and there is no legal principle or decision which compels me to hold, contrary to the fact, that the letter of the 8th of October is to be treated as communicated to the plaintiff on that day or on any day before the 20th, when the letter reached them. But before that letter had reached the plaintiffs they had accepted the offer, both by telegram and by post; and they had themselves resold the tin plates at a profit. In my opinion the withdrawal by the defendants on the 8th of October of their offer of the 1st was inoperative; and a complete contract binding on both parties was entered into on the 11th of October, when the plaintiffs accepted the offer of the 1st, which they had no reason to suppose had been withdrawn. Before leaving this part of the case it may be as well to point out the extreme injustice and inconvenience which any other conclusion would produce. If the defendants' contention were to prevail no person who had received an offer by post and had accepted it would know his position until he had waited such a time as to be quite sure that a letter withdrawing the offer had not been posted before his acceptance of it. It appears to me that both legal principles, and practical convenience require

> that a person who has accepted an offer not known to him to have been revoked, shall be in a position safely to act upon the footing that the offer and acceptance constitute a contract binding on both parties.

In contrast, the civil law countries adopt the reception theory, according to which the contract is concluded when the acceptance reaches the offeror. This is the solution now followed in France. The 2016 French reform clearly states in Art. 1122 that the contract is concluded when the acceptance is received by the offeror. Similar rules are followed in Germany, Italy, Spain, etc.

4.3 The battle of the forms

In contract negotiations the parties frequently make use of standard terms. In commercial transactions each party usually has its own terms, formulated in advance and for an indefinite number of contracts, in which they specify when, where and how the goods will be dispatched, how to proceed for payment, which law is applicable and so on.

The problem arises in the case of competing proposals contained within the parties' standard terms, in particular when they contain conflicting clauses. For example, we can imagine that one party offers to sell goods to the other party and the offer is contained in a standard form containing a clause according to which the transportation costs are at the offeree's charge and another clause determining that the applicable law is that of the offeror. The offeree accepts the offer through its own standard form, in which there is a clause according to which the cost of transport is included in the accepted price and that the applicable law is that of the offeree. This situation is referred to as the 'battle of forms'. The law has to decide which set of terms, if any, wins the 'battle' to govern the contract.

The solution given in the various legal systems is revealing of the different approaches described in the preceding pages of this book.

The civil law countries are reluctant to give effect to the terms of one of the parties, because it is clear that there is a divergence in their will. As a matter of fact, a formalistic approach would conclude that if the contract is concluded by conduct (i.e. after the acceptance the offeror simply dispatches the goods to the offeree) the applicable terms will be those of the offeree's because of the commonly accepted rule according to which if the acceptance is different from the offer it is considered as a counter-offer. So the conduct of the original offeror is in reality an acceptance of the offeree's counter-offer.

In France, this situation tends to be solved in the sense that where clauses found in the parties' standard terms are in conflict, the two provisions cancel each other out. This solution is now contained in Article 1119, according to which "where there is a conflict between the standard terms invoked by both parties the incompatible clauses shall be ineffective" ("en cas de discordance entre des condition générales invoquées par l'une et l'autre des parties, les clauses incompatibles sont sans effet").

The German civil code does not have a specific provision for this issue, but according to the general rules the solution is similar to the French one. More specifically, § 154 clearly provides that if the parties have not agreed on all points the contract is not entered into and § 155 refers to a hidden lack of agreement: when the parties to a contract which they consider to have been entered into have, in fact, not agreed on a point on which an agreement was required to be reached, whatever is agreed on is applicable if it is to be assumed that the contract would have been entered into even without a provision concerning this point. Moreover, § 306 specifies that when the standard terms have not become part of the contract or are ineffective, the contents of the contract are determined by the statutory provisions.

German Federal Supreme Court of Justice (Bundesgerichtshof) BGH 20 March 1985 is a good example of the German approach.[5]

On 27 October 1980, the debtor in bankruptcy ordered from the claimant clocks operating as time switches which were to be fitted into electrical stoves; the contract was subject to the general conditions of trade printed on the back of the claimant's order forms Under No 14; the order form states that changes in

5 BGH, 20 March 1985, NJW, 1985, p. 1838. The translation is adapted from the freely accessible website: https://law.utexas.edu/transnational/foreign-law-translations/german/case.php?id=1486.

the order must normally be in writing and that the purchasing conditions of the debtor in bankruptcy applied. No. 16 of these conditions states: "Differing conditions of trade. By accepting our order, the supplier agrees to our purchasing conditions. Where our order is confirmed by the supplier using conditions deviating therefrom, our conditions of purchase will continue exclusively to apply, even if we do not expressly raise any objections. Deviations will thus only apply where they have been expressly agreed by us in writing. If the supplier objects to this practice, he must immediately and specifically state his objections in a separate letter. In such cases we retain the right to cancel the order and no claims against us will result from such action. Our conditions will also apply for future transactions, even where they are not specifically referred to, as long as they have reached the customer in the course of an order confirmed by us."

On 11 February 1982, the debtor in bankruptcy placed with the claimant a follow-up order for the supply of further thermostats. The claimant confirmed the order referring to his General Conditions of Supply and Payment according to which his written confirmation of the order in conjunction with these Conditions were to apply exclusively. Any amendments or additions to the contractual clauses were only valid in written form; No. 7 of these general conditions contains an extended and expanded retention of proprietary rights for goods delivered. The claimant supplied the time switches and thermostats of a total value of DM 454 245.58. On 21 May 1982, the debtor in bankruptcy requested that conciliation proceedings be started. At that time, out of the above-mentioned and still unpaid deliveries he still had in stock switches not yet installed of a total value of DM 47 789.05 had already been installed in finished stoves which were still at the debtor's premises. During July/August 1982, the debtor in bankruptcy paid the equivalent price for the pieces which were not yet installed. On 29 October 1982, "follow up" bankruptcy proceedings were started in respect of the debtor's assets and the defendant appointed as receiver in bankruptcy. The claimant demanded from the defendant payment of the value of the appliances which, on 21 May 1982, had already been installed in stoves which were still with the bankrupt debtor. He also requested information as to what claims the bankrupt had on 21 May 1982 stemming from sales of stoves containing the switches and energy regulators supplied by him. The Landgericht rejected the claim. The claimant's appeal and further appeal were also unsuccessful.

The solution to the legal problem of the litigation depends on whether or not No. 7 of the General Conditions of Trade (AGB) had become part of the contract. If this is the case, the claimant's claim for payment can be justified on the basis of para. 46 of the Bankruptcy Order (Konkursordnung/KO) or on paras 989 et seq. BGB, para. 59 1 No. 1 KO or para. 812 et seq. BGB, para. 591 No. 4 KO [...]

Following the decision of the Landgericht, the court of appeal assumed that the claimant's General Conditions of Sale and Payment, and thus condition No. 7, had not become part of the contract. They had not been agreed upon by separate contract. A tacit inclusion into the contract is barred by the debtor's conditions of purchase known to the claimant. The defensive clauses contained in No. 16 of these conditions are not invalid according to para. 9 of the Act on General Conditions of Trade (AGB-Gesetz). By this clause, the debtor in bankruptcy intended to secure for all of his transactions as uniform contractual conditions as possible and especially to preclude suppliers' retention of title. This aim cannot be objected to, since any retention of title impedes at least any transfer of ownership by way of security which is normally linked to business arrangements for bank loans.

These arguments can withstand legal scrutiny, at least as far as their result is concerned.

a) In commercial business transactions, the inclusion of general conditions of trade in single contracts requires that the contractual partners tacitly or specifically agree on their application [...]. Without any legal error, the court of appeal has rejected the existence of an explicit agreement on the applicability of the claimant's general conditions of trade for this particular contract. The further appeal does not refute this argument. The court of appeal furthermore correctly assumed that the debtor in bankruptcy had not tacitly agreed to a total inclusion of the claimant's general conditions of trade. The assumption that the debtor in bankruptcy tacitly agreed to the claimant's conditions of sale is countermanded by the unequivocal statement contained in his conditions of purchase that he intended exclusively to conclude contracts according to his conditions and that differing conditions contained in a confirmation of orders will only apply once they have been agreed by him in writing. In this context it is irrelevant, whether or not the defensive clause has itself become part of the contract, a clause which was intended to make it clear during contractual discussions, i.e. before the contract was signed, that the purchaser will not be bound by any clauses contained in the seller's trading conditions except for those enumerated in the defensive clause itself. What matters is solely the debtor's intentions as expressed in the defensive clause after the claimant had confirmed the order, though with reference to his own general conditions and such change is not discernible from the facts of the case. As the appeal court assumes and the further appeal obviously does not dispute, in view of the – advance – objection to the application of the claimant's general conditions as explicitly stated in the debtor's defensive clause, and in the absence of other circumstances, such a change of intention cannot be thought to have taken place, especially not from the fact that the debtor failed once more to reject the claimant's conditions of sale and accepted the goods without reservation (see Senate, WM 1977, 451 (452)).

Without a contractual agreement between the partners concerning the claimant's conditions of sale, these have not altogether become part of the contract. The further appeal acknowledges this point.

b) However, the further appeal submits that the debtor in bankruptcy's defensive clause which bars a wholesale inclusion of the claimant's conditions of sale in the contract, does not preclude the fact that certain clauses of these conditions of sale have nonetheless become part of the contract. The defensive clause only excludes the claimant's conditions of sale in so far as these deviate from the debtor's purchasing conditions; it does not also exclude additional conditions to which the debtor had not expressly objected, such as No. 7 of the sales conditions containing rules on an extended retention of ownership with a clause on processing and advance assignment of rights, all the more where such additional conditions are customary for this particular line of business. The court cannot uphold this reasoning.

   aa) Where a contract, as here, has been concluded without agreement on the application of the general conditions of trade of one party, this does not mean that the corresponding optional legal rules automatically apply [...] in such a case and instead of the rules contained in the general conditions. From the intentions of the parties it can rather be deduced that such rules deviating from or supplementing optional legal rules will apply which have been set out in the general conditions of either party and where these conditions are of identical content and where their application has thus been intended by both parties.

bb) *such apparent consensus is however missing,* where one party's general conditions of trade contain "additional" rules which have no equivalent in the other party's conditions, such as – as here – the use of clauses on the retention of ownership. The question as to whether or not in such a case a tacit consent can be assumed of one party to the unilaterally fixed additional conditions of the other contractual partner, even where both parties' general conditions do not result in a consensus of intentions, can only be answered according to the intention of the party opposing the clause, in so far as this can be discerned from all other circumstances of the case [...]. In this case, no intention of the debtor in bankruptcy can be ascertained to indicate that his defensive clause was merely meant to exclude the claimant's sales conditions insofar as they run counter to his own conditions of purchase but not also other additional rules. By his defensive clause, the debtor clearly and unequivocally expressed his intention that for any orders placed only his own purchase conditions applied and that, without his expressed written acknowledgement, any other conditions would not become part of the contract even where he fails formally to object to them. *The debtor in bankruptcy thereby unequivocally expressed his intention* that his own conditions of purchase only leave room for the claimant's conditions of sale where and insofar as their contents are either identical with his own or where they have been agreed by him in writing [...]. There was therefore no need for the debtor to raise a specific objection against the retention of ownership clause contained in the claimant's conditions of sale in order to prevent the clause from becoming part of the contract.

English law adopts a different rule, the so-called 'last shot' analysis: victory goes to the party proposing its own terms as the final part of the sequence of terms, provided the other acquiesces.

This approach is well illustrated in the case of *Tekdata Intercommunications v Amphenol Ltd.* decided by the Court of Appeal in 2009.[6]

Amphenol supplied high specification materials to Tekdata, for eventual use in the construction of Rolls-Royce aero engines. Tekdata claimed that certain connectors were delivered late and were not fit for purpose or of merchantable quality. According to Tekdata, the contract of purchase was on the terms of their purchase orders (or, more accurately, revisions to purchase orders already placed). Amphenol defended by saying that the contracts were on the terms of their (Amphenol's) acknowledgement of the purchase orders and that those terms excluded or limited their liability for any breaches of contract. Applying the 'last shot' approach, the Court of Appeal accepted that Amphenol had made the last presentation of terms and Tekdata had acquiesced in these. Therefore, the exclusion clause contained in Amphenol's standard form had been incorporated.

Lord Justice Dyson

The so-called "last shot" doctrine has been explained in Chitty on Contracts (30th edition) at para 2-037 as meaning that where conflicting communications are exchanged, each is a counter-offer, so that if a contract results at all (eg from an acceptance by conduct) it must be on the terms of the final document in the series leading to the conclusion of the contract. This doctrine has been criticised in Anson's Law of Contract (28th edition) at p 39 as depending on chance and being potentially arbitrary as well as on the ground that, unless and until the counter-offer is accepted, there is no contract even though both buyer and seller may firmly believe that a contract has been made.

The paradigm battle of the forms occurs where A offers to buy goods from B on its (A's) conditions and B accepts the offer but

6 *Tekdata Interconnections Ltd v Amphenol Ltd* [2010] 2 All ER (Comm) 302, CA. Emphasis is added in order to attract attention on the relevant *dicta*.

only on its own conditions. As is pointed out in Cheshire, Fifoot & Furmston's Law of Contract (15th ed.) at p 210, it may be possible to analyse the legal situation that results as being that there is (i) a contract on A's conditions; (ii) a contract on B's conditions; (iii) a contract on the terms that would be implied by law, but incorporating neither A's nor B's conditions; (iv) a contract incorporating some blend of both parties' conditions; or (v) no contract at all.

In my judgment, *it is not possible to lay down a general rule that will apply in all cases where there is a battle of the forms. It always depends on an assessment of what the parties must objectively be taken to have intended. But where the facts are no more complicated than that A makes an offer on its conditions and B accepts that offer on its conditions and, without more, performance follows, it seems to me that the correct analysis is what Longmore LJ has described as the "traditional offer and acceptance analysis", i.e that there is a contract on B's conditions*. I accept that this analysis is not without its difficulties [...] But the rules which govern the formation of contracts have been long established and they are grounded in the concepts of offer and acceptance. So long as that continues to be the case, it seems to me that the general rule should be that the traditional offer and acceptance analysis is to be applied in battle of the forms cases. That has the great merit of providing a degree of certainty which is both desirable and necessary in order to promote effective commercial relationships.

In the present case, it was not contended on behalf of Amphenol that there was no contract between it and Tekdata. The issue was whose conditions were incorporated into the contract. On behalf of Tekdata, it is submitted that the acknowledgement of order by which Tekdata's offer was accepted "subject to the terms and conditions as printed overleaf" was in law an unqualified acceptance of Tekdata's offer (including its conditions). It is said that the words "subject to the terms and conditions as printed overleaf" were not intended to have, and did not in fact have, any contractual effect and were to be ignored.

In my judgment, such a conclusion could only be reached if Tekdata could show that the parties had expressly agreed that these words were to be ignored or if such an agreement was necessarily to be inferred from the circumstances of the case. I acknowledge that this is a high hurdle for Tekdata to surmount, but anything less would lead to an uncertainty which is inimical to commercial relationships.

Mr Chapple does not say that there was any express agreement that the words on the face of Amphenol's acknowledgement of order were to be ignored and the judge made no finding to that effect. Nor did the judge ask himself whether there were facts which gave rise to the necessary inference that this is what the parties must have agreed. He held the parties must have intended that Tekdata's conditions should apply for a number of reasons all of which were founded in what he described as "reasonable common sense" (para 19). At para 31, he said that it "would defy common sense in this particular commercial arrangement for the Amphenol terms and conditions to be party (sic) of any of these supplies". At para 56, he said that he justified his conclusion by reference to the context, the conduct of the parties in how they operated the contract "and one has to say that with the experience of a Mercantile Judge looking at how commercial parties in the aviation industry would behave and were behaving at this particular time."

I agree with the reasons given by Longmore LJ at [17] to [19] above that none of the factors relied on by the judge for concluding that Tekdata's conditions were incorporated justified his conclusion. Whether considered individually or in combination, they did not give rise to the necessary inference that the parties must have intended the words on the face of Amphenol's acknowledgement of order to have no effect and to contract on Tekdata's conditions.

In particular, the judge placed far too much reliance on the correspondence that was written after the dispute had arisen. I agree with Longmore LJ that post-contractual behaviour may be admissible to prove the terms of a contract. An obvious example is where there is an issue as to whether a term was orally agreed and in post-contractual correspondence the party who denies the existence of the term admits that it was agreed. But in a battle of the forms case where it is not suggested that there was any oral agreement as to which conditions should apply, I find it difficult to see how subsequent correspondence can shed light on the question of whose conditions were intended to apply, particularly, as Longmore LJ says, if the correspondence is written at the stage of trying to resolve a dispute. *The question of whose conditions were intended to apply must be determined objectively on the basis of the proper interpretation of the documents which comprise the contract viewed objectively in their context.* The focus must always be on what the parties must be taken, objectively, to have intended at the time when the contract was made. [...]

For these reasons as well as those given by Longmore LJ, I would allow this appeal.

It is worth noting that Dutch Law provides another solution, totally opposite to the English one and known as the 'first blow' rule: the terms and conditions of the offeror prevail, unless they are expressly rejected by the acceptor. Article 6:225 NW recites as follows:

1. The acceptance of an offer, made under different or additional conditions, is regarded as a new offer and as a rejection of the original offer.
2. Where a reply, that is intended as an acceptance, only differs from the offer on secondary issues, it will be a valid acceptance, which will form a binding agreement in accordance with the content of this acceptance, unless the offeror immediately objects to the differences.

3. Where offer and acceptance refer to the application of different standard terms and conditions, the second reference is without effect if it does not explicitly reject the application of the standard terms and conditions to which was referred firstly.[7]

The underlying idea is that it is up to the party making the last communication to solve the problem, clearly stating that the acceptance is contingent on the acceptance of its own terms and conditions.

In this context, the UNIDROIT Principles adopt an original approach, according to which the terms and conditions of both parties are included in the contract insofar as they can be reconciled, whereas the conflicting terms are left out.

Art. 2.1.22

Battle of forms

Where both parties use standard terms and reach agreement except on those terms, a contract is concluded on the basis of the agreed terms and of any standard terms which are common in substance unless one party clearly indicates in advance, or later and without undue delay informs the other party, that it does not intend to be bound by such a contract.

A not very dissimilar solution is adopted by PECL.

Art. 2:209

Conflicting General Conditions

(1) If the parties have reached agreement except that the offer and acceptance refer to conflicting general conditions of contract, a contract is nonetheless formed. The general

7 For this translation see http://dutchcivillaw.com/legislation/dcctitle6655.htm.

conditions form part of the contract to the extent that they are common in substance.

(2) However, no contract is formed if one party:

(a) has indicated in advance, explicitly, and not by way of general conditions, that it does not intend to be bound by a contract on the basis of paragraph (1); or

(b) without delay, informs the other party that it does not intend to be bound by such contract.

(3) General conditions of contract are terms which have been formulated in advance for an indefinite number of contracts of a certain nature, and which have not been individually negotiated between the parties.

5 Pre-contractual negotiations

The formation of a contract is often preceded by lengthy negotiations. Every legal system recognizes that the parties are free to enter into a negotiation and to abandon it, if they are not interested in going on. No one is obliged to continue a negotiation and conclude a contract against his or her will. At the same time, most legal systems accept a general duty of pre-contractual good faith. They consider that there is a 'grey zone' between the freedom to break off negotiations and the respect for the interest of the other party. In this 'grey zone' the parties must act in good faith. There are some forms of symptomatic conducts against the duty of good faith: when a party negotiates without having an intent to conclude a contract, when negotiations are broken off without any reason, when confidential information is disclosed to third persons. This is the civil law approach.

5.1 The civil law approach

The French civil code of 1804 did not contain a specific provision concerning the pre-contractual phase. However, very soon the courts started to extend to pre-contractual negotiations the application of Art. 1134, according to which contracts must be performed in good faith.

An interesting example of the approach followed by the French courts is the decision Cass. Civ., 3 October 1972.[1]

1 The original text is freely accessible through the following link: www.legifrance.gouv.fr/juri/id/JURITEXT000006988680/. The translation is provided by the author.

DOI: 10.4324/9781003251606-5

In the light of articles 1382 and 1383 civil code;

Whereas it emerges from the statements of the appealed judgment that the company "Residence Bonaparte" built a housing development in Ajaccio, having commercial areas at the ground floor;

Whereas Monoprix manifested the intention to buy the commercial areas if the company would have modified them according to the instructions given by its technicians;

Whereas the lengthy negotiations between the two companies were interrupted on the 7th December 1967 by Monoprix, having found another commercial area where to install its premises;

Whereas, having "Residence Bonaparte" sued Monoprix for damages resulting from the abusive interruption of negotiations, the appealed judgment rejected its request on the grounds that no intention to damage the company had been alleged, fixing the principle that "in the absence of a contrary agreement, the modifications to a property by his owner or done after his permission in order to adapt it to his needs are done at the owner's risk, so that the refusal to continue negotiations by the eventual buyer, even without a legitimate reason, do not engender his liability for damages". The rule would be different "if the eventual buyer intentionally asked for modifications only to create damages to the other party".

Whereas having so decided, the court of appeal violated the abovementioned articles, because liability can be affirmed also if the party has no intention to damage.

For these reasons, the judgment given by the court of appeal of Bastia is quashed and annulled and the case is referred to the court of appeal of Nimes.

After the 2016 reform, the new Art. 1112 provides that the conduct during negotiations has to fulfil the requirement of good faith. When the breach of negotiations is faulty, the other party is entitled to damages.[2]

In Germany, § 311 BGB, sec. 1, contains the general rule that, in principle, only a contract can create an obligation or alter the contents of an obligation. However, sec. 2 and 3 of the same § 311 prescribe that obligations can arise prior to the conclusion of a contract. These pre-contractual obligations are based on the protection of the other party's reliance arising when the parties initiate contacts with a view to concluding a contract and entering into negotiations. This relationship of reliance is at the origin of duties of care, protected by § 241 sec. 2, according to which "An obligation may also, depending on its contents, oblige each party to take account of the rights, legal interests and other interests of the other party".

Similarly, Article 1337 of the Italian civil code provides that during the course of negotiations the parties must act in good faith.

The UNIDROIT Principles 2 (.1.15) and the PECL follow the same approach. Art. 2.301 of the PECL prescribes: "A party is free to negotiate and is not liable for failure to reach an agreement. However, a party who has negotiated or broken off contrary to good faith is liable for the losses caused to the other party. It is contrary to good faith, in particular, for a party to enter into or continue negotiations with no real intention of reaching an agreement with the other party".

There are two decisive elements necessary for admitting a pre-contractual liability.

The first element is that negotiations need to have come to a point where the other party could reasonably expect that a contract would be concluded. This means that the mere hope of concluding the contract is not enough. There should be much more, such as lengthy negotiations, and the reliance has to be induced by the other party's conduct or declarations.

The second element is the absence of good reasons for breaking off the negotiations. This means that the other party should demonstrate, for instance, to have received a better offer from a third party, or that the counterparty did not act in good faith, for instance not disclosing some essential element.

2 "L'initiative, le déroulement et la rupture des négociations précontractuelles sont libres. Ils doivent impérativement satisfaire aux exigences de la bonne foi. En cas de faute commise dans les négociations, la réparation du préjudice qui en résulte ne peut avoir pour objet de compenser la perte des avantages attendus du contrat non conclu".

If the two elements described above are ascertained, a pre-contractual liability can arise and the other party is entitled to damages. The problem is to clarify the nature and extent of liability. In this respect, the main distinction is between reliance and expectation interest, sometimes referred to, respectively, as negative or positive interest. Recovery of the reliance (negative) interest means that the innocent party has the right to be reimbursed of all expenses incurred (travelling, preparing for meetings, staff involved, legal or scientific advice, etc.) and to recovery for lost opportunities (for example, concluding an alternative contract with a third party). The positive interest means that the innocent party has the right to recover the financial equivalent of what he or she would have had, had a valid contract been concluded, including the lost profit.

Most legal systems admit only the recovery of the negative interest. Article 1112-2 of the French code upholds the solution already adopted by case law and so it expressly excludes the loss of profits expected from contract and the loss of a chance of obtaining these, had the contract been concluded.

The position of Dutch law deserves attention, being quite original, admitting not only the negative, but also the positive interest.

Plas v Valburg is the leading case in Dutch law.[3]

The Municipal Council of the town of Valburg decided to build an indoor swimming pool, fixing the amount of HFL 1,312,000 for the construction costs, at a meeting held in June 1974. Four offers were submitted and the Council committee decided to ask Plas and another offeree to adapt their plans and submit priced tenders. Plas sought advice from external experts (a heating system consultant, an electricity consultant, a noise consultant and an architect), all at its own expense. In December 1974, Plas submitted an adapted offer priced HFL 1,300,000. It turned out that Plas had submitted the lowest price quotation and, accordingly, during a meeting the Mayor stated that Plas's tender was the lowest, that its plan was acceptable and that the Council would come to a decision about it, provided that only small further adjustments were introduced. During a subsequent meeting, where the issue of the swimming pool was not an item on the agenda, a Council member stated that another company had a plan for the construction of the

3 Hoge Raad 18 June 1982, NJ 1983, 723, note CJHB, *Plas v Municipality of Valburg*. For this translation: © H. Beale, B. Fauvarque-Cosson, J. Rutgers, S. Vogenauer, *Cases, Materials and Text on Contract Law*, 3rd ed., London, Hart Publishing, 2019, p. 461, an imprint of Bloomsbury Publishing plc.

swimming pool that was HFL 156,000 cheaper than Plas's plan. The Council decided to adopt this new plan and Plas brought an action seeking performance of an agreement which it submitted had been made. Alternatively, Plas claimed damages for default and, in a further alternative, for the breaking off of negotiations.

The District Court allowed his claim, but the Regional Court of Appeal set that judgment aside and dismissed all his claims. Plas appealed to the Hoge Raad, who allowed the appeal.

> 3.4 […] In the fourth of its grounds of judgment, the Regional Court of Appeal based its findings on the legal rule that the obligation to pay compensation on account of conduct in pre-contractual dealings which does not accord with the duty to act in good faith "extends no further than a requirement to make good the costs and damage incurred which the other party would not have suffered if the pre-contractual relationship had not arisen", and that it cannot therefore include an obligation to compensate for lost profits. However, the law generally affords no support for such a rule. It is not impossible that negotiations concerning a contract may reach such an advanced stage that the act of breaking them off must in itself be regarded, in the prevailing circumstances, as a breach of good faith, on the basis that the parties may be assumed mutually to have relied on the expectation that some sort of contract would in any event result from the negotiations. In such a situation, it may also be legitimate to find that an obligation exists to pay compensation for lost profits.
>
> 3.5 The fifth and sixth parts of the plea are directed against the fifth and sixth grounds on the judgement appealed against, in which the Regional Court of Appeal held that no compensation was payable in respect of the costs and damage incurred by Plas prior to the discussion on 9 January 1975, because it followed from Plas' arguments that the pre-contractual relationship on which his claim for compensation was based arose in

> the course of, and as a result of, that discussion, and because Plas never maintained that the Council was not free, prior to that date, to withdraw from the negotiations. [...] The Regional Court of Appeal's finding that Plas at no time asserted that the Council was not free, prior to 9 January 1975, to withdraw from the negotiations must be considered in conjunction with the District Court's ruling that, following the discussion on that date, the Council was no longer entitled to break off the negotiations. In omitting to deal with the objection raised against that ruling by the Council, the Regional Court of Appeal clearly assumed that the ruling in question was correct. However, if the Council was no longer able, after 9 January 1975, to withdraw from the negotiations, it is impossible to see why a breach of its obligations should not result in the Council being required to make good costs which had already been incurred before 9 January 1975 in the context of the negotiations held prior to that date. Such a requirement to pay compensation might even arise if the negotiations had not yet reached the stage at which the Council was no longer able in good faith to break them off but had nevertheless already advanced to the point that the act of breaking them off resulted, in the circumstances, in its no longer being free to walk away from them without assuming responsibility, wholly or in part, for the expenses incurred by Plas.

Hence, in Dutch law one can discern three successive stages in the pre-contractual phase and their respective liability schemes: (i) each party is free to break off the negotiation without facing the risk of being obliged to compensate the cost incurred by the other party; (ii) each party is free to break off the negotiation but there is an obligation to compensate the cost incurred by the other party; (iii) each party does not have the freedom to break off the negotiation, since it is contrary to the principle of good faith. The party who breaks off will be obligated to pay compensation for the cost incurred by the other party and even, under certain circumstances, to pay compensation for the cost incurred by the other party and for loss of expected profit suffered by the other party.

Moreover, aside from the obligation to pay compensation for the cost incurred by the other party and for loss of expected profit suffered by the other party, a party may be compelled by the court to continue the negotiation in order to come to a concluded contract. However, this outcome is controversial.

Plas v Valburg is certainly a leading case, introducing a profound change in Dutch law, but its implementation in subsequent cases is not very clear. The rule has been refined as follows: a liability will arise in a broken off negotiation if (i) a party (who misses out on the contract) might reasonably expect that that kind of a contract will emanate from the negotiation or (ii) it is unjustifiable in connection with other circumstances. A liability as a result of a broken off negotiation should not be easily assumed.

To conclude, the Dutch example clearly shows that it is difficult to draw a precise line to ascertain when breaking off negotiations proves to be illegal. In particular, in the Dutch solution the boundaries between the no-contract sphere and the conclusion of contract tend to be vague and obscure.

5.2 English law

Against this background, the position of English law is significantly different. English courts do not recognize a general doctrine of fault in bargaining, nor a general doctrine of good faith negotiation. Traditionally, English lawyers regard good faith as too vague a concept. Moreover, the need to protect commerce has always been seen as implying that the parties who engage in negotiations do it at their own risk and during the negotiations they are free to interrupt them until the contract is concluded. In short, English law is reluctant to admit any liability during negotiations.

The English leading case is *Walford v Miles*. It makes clear that English law does not recognize a duty of good faith in negotiations.[4] This decision has been criticized on the grounds that it does not impose a sanction on a party who negotiates in bad faith but does not make any misrepresentations.[5] Currently, there are many signs that members of the judiciary are more receptive to the idea that good faith should have a role to play in English contract

4 *Waldorf v Miles* [1992] 2 AC 128. Emphasis is added in order to attract attention on the most relevant *dicta*.

5 In this sense, Lord Steyn, 'Contract Law: Fulfilling the Reasonable Expectations of Honest Man', *LQR*, 1997, 113, p. 433, especially at p. 439.

law, due also to the influence of European law. The requirement of good faith as enacted in many Regulations is now part of English law, for instance under the Consumer Rights Act (especially Part 2). Some commentators argue that the influence of this concept should extend broadly, being not limited to the particular context of the applicable legislation.[6] This issue continues to be debated. Nevertheless, as far as the pre-contractual stage is concerned, the position of English law is clear-cut: the parties are free to abandon the negotiations without incurring in any liability.

Lord Ackner

My Lords, Mr. Martin Walford, the first named appellant, is a solicitor in private practice. He is the brother of the second named appellant, Mr. Charles Walford, who is a chartered accountant. They own the third named plaintiff, a company which plays no part in this dispute. The respondents, Mr. and Mrs. Miles, husband and wife, at the material time owned a company P.N.M. Laboratories Ltd., together with premises in Blackfriars Road, London, which was let to the company where it carried on a photographic processing business. The company's auditors at the material time were Mr. Patel and Mr. Khanderia who carried on their profession under the name of Patel, Khanderia & Co.

In 1985 because of illness, Mr. Miles decided to sell the company and its business premises. Negotiations took place with Mr. Patel and Mr. Khanderia via the medium of a company, Statusguard Ltd., in which Mr. Patel and Mr. Khanderia had a 30 per cent. interest. These negotiations proved unsuccessful.

Towards the end of 1986, Mr. and Mrs. Miles decided once more to try to sell the company and its business premises. Mr. Patel put forward an offer of £1.9m. Meanwhile the Walfords had heard that the business was up for sale. There

6 R. Brownsword, *Contract Law. Themes for the Twenty-First Century*, 2nd ed., Oxford University Press, Oxford, 2006, pp. 123 ff.

was a meeting between Mr. Martin Walford and Mr. Miles on 23 April 1987. Although the Walfords knew nothing about the photographic processing business, they thought they had found a bargain. The Miles were prepared to warrant that at the date of completion the cash resources in the company's bank account would not be less than £1m. and that the trading profits for the 12 months following completion would not be less than £300,000 before tax. The Walfords considered that the business and its premises were in the words of Mr. Naughton in opening this appeal, "dramatically undervalued." They were accordingly enthusiastic to purchase it at this price. Following a meeting on 12 March 1987 at Mr. Martin Walford's offices, the main terms of the purchase were agreed in principle and on 16 March Mr. Martin Walford faxed a letter expressly headed "subject to contract" to Mr. Randall of Messrs. Tarlo Lyons Randall Rose, the solicitor for Mr. and Mrs. Miles. The purchasers were not to be the Walfords but a company controlled by them (the third named appellant). In his letter of 16 March Mr. Martin Walford recorded that Mr. Miles had given his assurance that, provided he received a clear indication of the intention to proceed with the purchase not later than the close of business on Wednesday, 25 March, he would not treat with any third party or consider any other alternative offers. Mr. Randall replied on 17 March that he did not have any instructions to proceed with the sale and that Mr. Miles had not given the assurance alleged. This letter was however overtaken by oral exchanges which occurred on the same day between Mr. Martin Walford and Mr. Miles. On 18 March Mr. Martin Walford wrote to Mr. Randall confirming what had been agreed during that telephone conversation. It is common ground that the penultimate paragraph of that letter correctly sets out the agreement which had been reached as to negotiations between third parties. It reads as follows:

"The last matter discussed between Mr. Miles and me related to our ability to make payment for the shares in the business and the property. He asked me to provide a comfort letter from our bankers confirming that they are, subject to contract, prepared to provide the finance of £2,000,000 to enable Acquisition Corpn. to effect the purchase. Mr. Miles agreed that if such a letter were in your hands by close of business on Friday of this week he would terminate negotiations with any third party or consideration of any alternative with a view to concluding agreements with me and my brother and Acquisition Corpn. and he further agreed that even if he received a satisfactory proposal from any third party before close of business on Friday night he would not deal with that third party and nor would he give further consideration to any alternative."

The letter from Lloyds Bank which Mr. Walford enclosed, dated 18 March, was addressed to Mr. Randall and expressed to be given without responsibility. It confirmed that the bank had offered the brothers loan facilities to enable them and the company controlled by them to make the purchase for £2m.

On 25 March Mr. Randall wrote to Mr. Martin Walford acknowledging the receipt of this letter and enclosure, and confirmed that, subject to contract, his client agreed to the sale of the property and the shares at a total price of £2m. On the same day, Mr. Randall wrote to Mr. Patel's solicitors informing them that his client had concluded terms for the sale of the property and the shares in the company to another party and that he was waiting to receive a draft contract. He pointed out that everything was still subject to contract and that the transaction might not go through, but that if it did not, his client would be interested to pursue discussions. On 26 March Mr. Walford's solicitors sent preliminary inquiries and a draft share purchase agreement to Mr. Randall, who sent them on to Mr. Miles the following day. Mr. Martin Walford was anxious to meet Mr. Miles upon that day, but Mr. Miles was not available.

On 30 March Mr. Randall wrote to Mr. Martin Walford informing him that, after careful consideration, his clients had decided to sell to a company associated with the auditors, adding that he hoped that the Walfords would accept his clients' decision without question. This they refused to do. They treated Mr. Randall's letter as a repudiation of what they alleged to be a contract and then issued these proceedings. Meanwhile the shares in the company and the property in Blackfriars Road had been sold for £2m. to Statusguard Ltd., the corporate vehicle through which Mr. Patel and Mr. Khanderia had tried to make the purchase in 1985.

Mr. Miles did not give evidence before the trial judge, His Honour Judge Bates Q.C. sitting as a judge of the High Court. It was Mrs. Miles who informed the court that she and her husband spent the afternoon of Friday 27 March at the company's premises and during that time decided not to sell to the Walfords or their company. Her explanation was that they were concerned whether they and their staff would get on well with Mr. Martin Walford. If they failed to do so, they might lose staff and then fail to produce the £300,000 profit which was the subject of the warranty. Moreover, they were both concerned that her husband's health might suffer during the year that he would be continuing to work in the business, providing the Walfords with the expertise which they lacked. They therefore decided, either to continue in business themselves or to ask Mr. Patel if he was still interested. There was a telephone conversation on the evening of Friday, 27 March with Mr. Patel, who confirmed that he was still interested and agreed readily to increase his offer by £100,000, thus matching the price which the Walfords had offered. Mr. Patel, in his evidence, said that after he had received Mr. Randall's letter of 25 March he had no contact with Mr. Miles until the telephone conversation on 27 March, to which I have just referred. The trial judge did not believe him.

He concluded that Mr. Miles and Mr. Patel had continued to keep in touch, notwithstanding the oral agreement of 17 March recorded in the letter of 18 March.

The pleaded case

The Walfords relied upon an oral agreement, collateral to the negotiations which were proceeding, to purchase the company and the land it occupied "subject to contract." The consideration for this oral agreement was twofold—firstly the Walfords agreeing to continue the negotiations and not to withdraw and secondly, their providing the comfort letter from their bankers in the terms requested.

For this consideration it was alleged in paragraph 5 of the statement of claim as follows:

> "the first defendant on behalf of himself and the second defendant would terminate negotiations with any third party or consideration of any alternative with a view to concluding an agreement with the Plaintiffs and further that even if he received a satisfactory proposal from any third party prior to the close of business on 25 March 1987, he would not deal with that third party or give further consideration to any alternative."

As thus pleaded, the agreement purported to be what is known as a "lock-out" agreement, providing the plaintiffs with an exclusive opportunity to try and come to terms with the defendants, but without expressly providing any duration for such an opportunity.

For reasons which will become apparent hereafter, it was decided to amend this paragraph by the following addition:

> "It was a term of the said collateral agreement necessarily to be implied to give business efficacy thereto that,

> so long as they continued to desire to sell the said property and shares, the first defendant on behalf of himself and the second defendant would continue to negotiate in good faith with the plaintiff."

Thus the statement of claim alleged that, not only were the defendants "locked-out" for some unspecified time from dealing with any third party, but were "locked-in" to dealing with the plaintiffs, also for an unspecified period.

In the statement of claim it was further alleged that by reason of the wrongful repudiation by the Miles, the Walfords lost the opportunity of completing the sale and purchase of the shares and property, and that the true market value of the shares and the property was of the order of £3m. Accordingly the Walfords claimed that they lost the difference between the price which they had agreed to pay of £2m. and the true market value. In addition to the above, there was a claim for damages for misrepresentation by the Miles in continuing to deal with third parties. This consisted of the expenses incurred in the negotiations and in the preparation of contract documents.

The decision of first instance and the Court of Appeal

After the close of pleadings, directions were given, inter alia, that the assessment of any damages to which the Walfords might be entitled for the alleged loss of opportunity of completing the sale and purchase of the shares and property should await the determination of the issue of liability. At the trial it was contended on behalf of the Miles that the agreement alleged in paragraph 5 of the amended statement of claim was no more than an agreement to negotiate and as such was unenforceable. The judge did not deal with this contention. He held that there was a collateral agreement whereby the Miles undertook to terminate negotiations with any third party or consideration of any alternative and that, even if Mr. Miles received a satisfactory proposal from any third party before the close of business on the Friday night, he would not deal with that party or give further consideration to any alternative, and that this agreement had been repudiated by the Miles. He therefore ordered that the damages for the alleged loss of opportunity be assessed. He further held that the promises of Mr. Miles under the collateral agreement were misrepresentations and awarded the Walfords £700 on account of special damages, being the agreed wasted expenditure.

In the Court of Appeal, by a majority (Dillon and Stocker L.JJ.) the appeal was allowed (save to the extent of the award of the damages for misrepresentation) on the grounds that the agreement alleged was no more than an agreement to negotiate and was therefore unenforceable. Bingham L.J. who dissented, would have held that the agreement was enforceable on the ground that it could be construed as an agreement by the Miles not to deal with any party other than the Walfords and not to entertain any alternative proposal. He would have set aside the award of damages for misrepresentation on the grounds that it was not justified by the evidence or the trial judge's findings. Before your Lordships the respondents were not contesting the £700 award.

The validity of the agreement alleged in paragraph 5 of the statement of claim as amended

The justification for the implied term in paragraph 5 of the amended statement of claim was that in order to give the collateral agreement "business efficacy", Mr. Miles was obliged to "continue to negotiate in good faith." [...]

Mr. Naughton [the appellant's lawyer, ndr] accepted that as the law now stands and has stood for approaching 20 years, an agreement to negotiate is not recognised as an enforceable contract. This was first decided in terms in *Courtney & Fairbairn Ltd. v. Tolaini Brothers (Hotels) Ltd.* [1975] 1 W.L.R. 297, where Lord Denning M.R. said, at pp. 301–302:

> If the law does not recognise a contract to enter into a contract (when there is a fundamental term yet to be agreed) it seems to me it cannot recognise a contract to negotiate. The reason is because it is too uncertain to have any binding force … It seems to me that a contract to negotiate, like a contract to enter into a contract, is not a contract known to the law … I think we must apply the general principle that where there is a fundamental matter left undecided and to be the subject of negotiation, there is no contract.

Before your Lordships it was sought to argue that the decision in Courtney's case [1975] 1 W.L.R. 297 was wrong. Although the cases in the United States did not speak with one voice your Lordships' attention was drawn to the decision of the United States' Court of Appeal, Third Circuit, in *Channel Home Centers, Division of Grace Retail Corporation v. Grossman* (1986) 795 F. 2d 291 as being "the clearest example" of the American cases in the appellants' favour. That case raised the issue whether an agreement to negotiate in good faith, if supported by consideration, is an enforceable contract. I do not find the decision of any assistance. While accepting that an agreement to agree is not an enforceable contract, the Court of Appeal appears to have proceeded on the basis that an agreement to negotiate in good faith is synonymous with an agreement to use best endeavours and as the latter is enforceable, so is the former. This appears to me, with respect, to be an unsustainable proposition. *The reason why an agreement to negotiate, like an agreement to agree, is unenforceable, is simply because it lacks the necessary certainty. The same does not apply to an agreement to use best endeavours. This uncertainty is demonstrated in the instant case by the provision which it is said has to be implied in the agreement for the determination of the negotiations. How can a court be expected to decide whether, subjectively, a proper reason existed for the termination of negotiations? The answer suggested depends upon whether the negotiations have been determined "in good faith." However the concept of a duty to carry on negotiations in good faith is inherently repugnant to the adversarial position of the parties when involved in negotiations. Each party to the negotiations is entitled to pursue his (or her) own interest, so long as he avoids making misrepresentations. To advance that interest he must be entitled, if he thinks it appropriate, to threaten to withdraw from further negotiations or to withdraw in fact, in the hope that the opposite party may seek to reopen the negotiations by offering him improved terms.* Mr. Naughton, of course, accepts that the agreement upon which he relies does not contain a duty to complete the negotiations. But that still leaves the vital question – how is a vendor ever to know that he is entitled to withdraw from further negotiations? How is the court to police such an "agreement?" A duty to negotiate in good faith is as unworkable in practice as it is inherently inconsistent with the position of a negotiating party. It is here that the uncertainty lies. In my judgment, while negotiations are in existence either party is entitled to withdraw from those negotiations, at any time and for any reason. There can be thus no obligation to continue to negotiate until there is a "proper reason" to withdraw. Accordingly a bare agreement to negotiate has no legal content. […]

I would accordingly dismiss this appeal with costs.

As we can see, "the concept of a duty to carry on negotiations in good faith is inherently repugnant to the adversarial positions of the parties when involved in negotiations" and "while negotiations are in existence either party is entitled to withdraw from those negotiations, at any time and for any reason".

Cobbe v Yeoman's Row Management Ltd. is another interesting case, well known also for other important *dicta*.[7]

The claimant, an experienced property developer, made an oral agreement with the third defendant, the sole director of the first defendant's company, to purchase for £12m a property comprising a number of flats, of which the first defendant was the registered freehold proprietor, for redevelopment into six town houses. The arrangement was that the first defendant would obtain vacant possession of the property and the claimant would develop it and keep any profit subject to overage under which each party would have 50% of the gross proceeds of the property over £24m. Encouraged by the third defendant on behalf of the first defendant and acting in the belief that the property would be sold to him, the claimant spent the next 18 months engaging architects and other professionals as well as applying for planning permission. Immediately after the grant of planning permission the defendants withdrew from the agreement, demanded £20m as the price for the sale of the freehold and suggested that the first defendant should receive 40% of the amount by which the gross proceeds exceeded £40m. The claimant brought proceedings alleging, inter alia, that the defendants were estopped from denying that he had acquired a beneficial interest in the property because they had acted unconscionably in knowingly inducing and encouraging by their actions his belief, on which he had relied to his detriment, that the property would be sold to him and then refusing to honour the oral agreement. Alternatively that there was a constructive trust in his favour. The judge found that the third defendant on behalf of the first defendant had encouraged the claimant's belief that if he succeeded in obtaining planning permission the oral agreement would be honoured and that he had taken unconscionable advantage of him. He concluded that the claims concerning proprietary estoppel and constructive trust succeeded. The Court of Appeal dismissed the defendants' appeal.

The speech of Lord Scott of Foscote is particularly interesting (no. 91 ff.).

7 [2008] 1 WLR 1752.

> When examined in that way, Mr Cobbe's case seems to me to fail on the simple but fundamental point that, as persons experienced in the property world, both parties knew that there was no legally binding contract, and that either was therefore free to discontinue the negotiations without legal liability—that is, liability in equity as well as at law. [...] Mr Cobbe was therefore running a risk, but he stood to make a handsome profit if the deal went ahead, and the market stayed favourable. He may have thought that any attempt to get Mrs Lisle-Mainwaring to enter into a written contract before the grant of planning permission would be counter-productive. Whatever his reasons for doing so, the fact is that he ran a commercial risk, with his eyes open, and the out-come has proved unfortunate for him. It is true that he did not expressly state, at the time, that he was relying solely on Mrs Lisle-Mainwaring's sense of honour, but to draw that sort of distinction in a commercial context would be as unreal-istic, in my opinion, as to draw a firm distinction depending on whether the formula "subject to contract" had or had not actually been used.

The total rejection of resorting to the concept of good faith does not mean that English law never protects a party to negotiations. Sometimes, other doctrines can be helpful, such as the unjust enrichment relief. For example, in the *British steel* case the claimant had delivered a large number of special 'steel nodes' for use by the defendant construction company in erecting a building.[8] All the nodes had been supplied, but the defendant claimed that they were delivered too slowly and in the wrong sequence. As a result, the defendant claimed to have suffered delay in completing its project. The dispute concerns both the main claim for payment and the defendant's counterclaim for compensation in respect of the defendant's commercial

8 *British Steel Corporation v Cleveland Bridge and Engineering Company* [1984] 1 All ER 504.

loss caused by the alleged slow and haphazard delivery of these materials. The Judge (Goff J) held that no contract had arisen both because the parties did not reach consensus on the price to be paid and because there remained an unresolved issue concerning the supplier's possible liability for consequential loss. A letter of intent was considered to be irrelevant, but the Judge recognized, on the basis of restitution, an extra-contractual cause of action, because it was certain that the goods were not delivered as a present. This case shows that restitution can be a valid alternative to good faith in order to give relief in cases of pre-contractual liability. Of course, this is true only for cases where one party delivered goods in the absence of a contract, but it is of no help when the party was deceived by the breaking off of the counter party.

5.3 Other common law jurisdictions: the example of Australian law

In contrast with English law, other common law jurisdictions adopt a more nuanced approach towards pre-contractual liability. For instance, in the United States, current contract law theory still denies the existence of a duty of good faith in negotiation and neither the UCC nor the Restatement imposes a duty of good faith in the negotiation of contracts. Nevertheless, bad faith in negotiation may give rise to sanctions under the doctrine of promissory estoppel or other theories.[9]

An interesting example showing that the rigidity of English law was tempered in other common law jurisdictions comes from the Australian's case *Walton Stores (Interstate) Ltd v Maher*.[10]

9 S. J. Burton, E. G. Andersen, *Contractual Good Faith: Formation, Performance, Breach, Enforcement*, Little, Brown and Company, Boston , 1995, § 8.2.2. For a general overview, see N. E. Nedzel, 'A Comparative Study of Good Faith, Fair Dealing, and Precontractual Liability', *Tul. Eur.. & Civ. L. F.* 1997, 12, p. 97. More recently, also for a comparative account of English and US laws, cf. C. Perry, 'Good Faith in English and US Contract Law: Divergent Theories, Practical Similarities', *Bus. L. Int'l* 2016, 17, p. 27.

10 (1988) 164 CLR 387. Emphasis is added in order to attract attention on the most relevant *dicta*.

Brennan J.

1. In October and early November 1983, officers and agents of Waltons Stores (Interstate) Ltd. ("Waltons") were negotiating with Mr and Mrs Maher for the construction by the Mahers of store premises on land which they owned in Nowra to be leased to Waltons. Mr Roth of Dawson Waldron was the solicitor for Waltons and Mr Elvy of Morton & Harris was the solicitor for the Mahers. They adopted an unusual conveyancing procedure. A draft Deed of Agreement for Lease was to be drawn by the lessee's solicitor Mr Roth and, when the terms were agreed, an exchange of contracts was to be effected. Time was short. Waltons specified 15 January 1984 as the date by which the store building was to be available for fitting out and 5 February 1984 as the date by which the store building was to be completed. Waltons had sold their store premises in Nowra and were required to vacate those premises by mid-January 1984. The contract between Waltons and the Mahers needed to be concluded in time to allow Mr Maher to meet the specified dates for fitting out and completion. The work to be done by Mr Maher included the demolition of a substantial structure on the site before the erection of the store building could be commenced. On 7 November 1983, Mr Elvy told Mr Roth that "the agreement must be concluded within the next day or two otherwise it will be impossible for Maher to complete it". At that time, Mr Elvy was seeking some amendments to the draft Deed of Agreement for Lease. Although the amendments had been agreed as between the solicitors, Waltons had not then given its final approval. In addition, a schedule of finishes was required for annexure to the Deed.

On 7 November, after Mr Elvy spoke to Mr Roth, Mr Roth wrote to Mr Elvy enclosing a redrafted Deed of Agreement for Lease which incorporated, to the extent necessary, all the amendments on which he and Mr Elvy had agreed. Mr Roth wrote:

> You should note that we have not yet obtained our client's specific instructions to each amendment requested, but we believe that approval will be forthcoming. We shall let you know tomorrow if any amendments are not agreed to.
>
> We also believe that a Schedule of Finishes should be annexed to the Deed prior to exchange.

Mr Roth did not inform Mr Elvy, either "tomorrow" or at any later time, that the amendments had not been agreed to.

2. Mr Elvy accordingly had his clients execute the Deed and prepare and sign a schedule of finishes. He sent these documents to Mr Roth on 11 November under cover of this letter:

> We thank you for your letter of the 7th November and now return amended counterpart Deed of Agreement for Lease signed by our clients, by way of exchange. Would you kindly forward the original Deed executed by your client.
>
> We enclose also Schedule of Finishes signed by our clients together with a copy thereof for approval and annexure to the Deed and two (2) copies of the floor plan for annexure to the copy lease annexed to the Deed, prior to exchange.
>
> When returning the executed Deed you might forward to us a cheque in the sum of $2000.20 in order that we may attend to stamping of the Deed.

(It will be convenient hereafter to adopt the terminology of this letter, describing the document forwarded by Mr Elvy "by way of exchange" as the counterpart Deed and the document to be executed by Waltons as the original Deed). When Mr Elvy wrote this letter, he thought it was his responsibility to attend to the stamping of the original and counterpart Deeds. Subsequently he realized that that was Mr Roth's responsibility. If Mr Elvy had been responsible for stamping the original and counterpart Deeds, presumably both would have been sent to him after Waltons had executed the original Deed; if Mr Roth had been responsible for stamping the original and counterpart Deeds, presumably Mr Elvy would have had to return the executed original Deed for stamping after it had been delivered to him by way of exchange. The implications of the conveyancing procedure adopted by the solicitors were the subject of an important finding by the learned trial judge to which reference will presently be made. Mr Elvy's letter and the enclosures were received by Mr Roth on or about 14 November. Mr Roth did not deliver the original Deed executed by Waltons to Mr Elvy as he had requested. Waltons did not execute the Deed. Mr Elvy made no enquiry to find out when the executed original Deed would be delivered to him. Nor did Mr Roth return the counterpart Deed until it was sent accompanied by a letter dated 19 January 1984 which Mr Roth then wrote on his client's instructions. (He had not communicated with Mr Elvy since 11 November 1983.) The letter of 19 January 1984 read:

> We refer to your letter of 11th November 1983 and regret to inform you that our client has instructed us that it does not intend to proceed with this transaction. We apologise for any inconvenience caused, and return the Deed of Agreement for Lease and

> Schedule of Finishes signed by your clients. The copies of the floor plan are also enclosed.

The contents of this letter reached Mr Maher on 22 or 23 January 1984. By that time, Mr Maher had demolished the structure which had been standing on the site, had poured two-fifths of the concrete slab and had laid sixty to seventy per cent of the brickwork required to build a store in accordance with Waltons' requirements. Mr Maher had put this work in hand shortly after he received Mr Elvy's letter of advice dated 14 November 1983:

> We refer to the writer's recent several attendances on Mr. Maher, and confirm that the amended Agreement for Lease duly executed by you both has been forwarded to the Lessee's Solicitors for execution by the Lessor and exchange of Agreement.
>
> We note that you will commence work in accordance with the Agreement for Lease immediately as the work to be completed by you on the property is required to be completed on or by the 5th February 1984.
>
> In the event that for any reason the Lessors work is not completed by the 31st March 1984, the Lessee may by notice in writing rescind the Agreement.
>
> Following return of the exchanged Agreement we shall arrange for the same to be stamped.

3. Mr Elvy wrote this letter, as the text shows, without having received the original Deed executed by Waltons. In his evidence, Mr Maher said in reference to his solicitor's letter to him:

> In my thinking it confirmed that everything was proceeding correctly and on receipt of that I ordered the

> Kato Excavators to demolish the rather substantial building which was in very very good order.

The reason why Mr Maher commenced the work was his expectation that a binding agreement would be brought into existence. As he said:

> We took for granted they would complete their part of the bargain and we duly set all our efforts into motion to do the job for them, in the limited time that was available to us.

Mr Maher expected that execution and delivery of the original Deed would take place [...].

4. The evidence revealed why Waltons withdrew from the arrangement and why time had been allowed to pass before Mr Roth advised Mr Elvy of Waltons' decision. Mr Rose, a property consultant who was retained by Waltons, had given Mr Roth instructions "to go slow on the transaction". Mr Rose explained "that meant that we did not want to get ourselves into a legally binding position". The reason for these instructions lay in a marketing report which suggested a need for Waltons to change its retailing strategy in a number of country centres including Nowra. That report was under consideration by the directors of Waltons and, as no decision had been made on whether to proceed to lease the proposed building, Mr Rose "did not want anything done to jeopardize the potential contractual situation between Waltons and Mahers". He was seeking to keep the arrangements with the Mahers on foot until a decision was made by Waltons.
5. Waltons knew that Mr Maher was proceeding with the building. On 10 December 1983, the manager of the Waltons store in Nowra reported to his group manager that demolition work had commenced on the site. By 10 or 11 January

1984, Waltons' officers knew that Mr Maher was proceeding with construction. Nobody had told Mr Maher that Waltons had had a change of heart. Although Mr Gosling, who was the property manager for Waltons in New South Wales, gave evidence that he had doubts whether the building under construction was being built for Waltons, he admitted that he did not try to resolve those doubts. The only reasonable inference open on the evidence is that Waltons knew that Mr Maher was building the store in conformity with the terms of the Deed which he had executed.

6. After Waltons refused to proceed in the transaction, Mr and Mrs Maher commenced proceedings in the Supreme Court of New South Wales [...]

23. *Parties who are negotiating a contract may proceed in the expectation that the terms will be agreed and a contract made but, so long as both parties recognize that either party is at liberty to withdraw from the negotiations at any time before the contract is made, it cannot be unconscionable for one party to do so. Of course, the freedom to withdraw may be fettered or extinguished by agreement but, in the absence of agreement, either party ordinarily retains his freedom to withdraw. It is only if a party induces the other party to believe that he, the former party, is already bound and his freedom to withdraw has gone that it could be unconscionable for him subsequently to assert that he is legally free to withdraw.*

24. It is essential to the existence of an equity created by estoppel that the party who induces the adoption of the assumption or expectation knows or intends that the party who adopts it will act or abstain from acting in reliance on the assumption or expectation: see per Lord Denning M.R. in *Crabb v. Arun District Council*, at p 188. When the adoption of an assumption or expectation is induced by the making of a promise, the knowledge or intention that the assumption or

expectation will be acted upon may be easily inferred. But if a party encourages another to adhere to an assumption or expectation already formed or acquiesces in the making of an assumption or the entertainment of an expectation when he ought to object to the assumption or expectation – steps which are tantamount to inducing the other to adopt the assumption or expectation – the inference of knowledge or intention that the assumption or expectation will be acted on may be more difficult to draw.

25. The unconscionable conduct which it is the object of equity to prevent is the failure of a party, who has induced the adoption of the assumption or expectation and who knew or intended that it would be relied on, to fulfil the assumption or expectation or otherwise to avoid the detriment which that failure would occasion. The object of the equity is not to compel the party bound to fulfil the assumption or expectation; it is to avoid the detriment which, if the assumption or expectation goes unfulfilled, will be suffered by the party who has been induced to act or to abstain from acting thereon.
26. If this object is kept steadily in mind, the concern that a general application of the principle of equitable estoppel would make non-contractual promises enforceable as contractual promises can be allayed. A non-contractual promise can give rise to an equitable estoppel only when the promisor induces the promisee to assume or expect that the promise is intended to affect their legal relations and he knows or intends that the promisee will act or abstain from acting in reliance on the promise, and when the promisee does so act or abstain from acting and the promisee would suffer detriment by his action or inaction if the promisor were not to fulfil the promise. When these elements are present, equitable estoppel almost wears the appearance of contract, for the action or inaction of the promisee looks like

consideration for the promise on which, as the promisor knew or intended, the promisee would act or abstain from acting. [...].

27. But there are differences between a contract and an equity created by estoppel. A contractual obligation is created by the agreement of the parties; an equity created by estoppel may be imposed irrespective of any agreement by the party bound. A contractual obligation must be supported by consideration; an equity created by estoppel need not be supported by what is, strictly speaking, consideration. The measure of a contractual obligation depends on the terms of the contract and the circumstances to which it applies; the measure of an equity created by estoppel varies according to what is necessary to prevent detriment resulting from unconscionable conduct. [...]

32. The qualifications proposed bring the principle closer to a principle the object of which is to avoid detriment occasioned by non-fulfilment of the promise. But the better solution of the problem is reached by identifying the unconscionable conduct which gives rise to the equity as the leaving of another to suffer detriment occasioned by the conduct of the party against whom the equity is raised. Then *the object of the principle can be seen to be the avoidance of that detriment and the satisfaction of the equity calls for the enforcement of a promise only as a means of avoiding the detriment and only to the extent necessary to achieve that object.* So regarded, equitable estoppel does not elevate non-contractual promises to the level of contractual promises and the doctrine of consideration is not blown away by a side-wind. Equitable estoppel complements the tortious remedies of damages for negligent mis-statement or fraud and enhances the remedies available to a party who acts or abstains from acting in reliance on what another induces him to believe.

6 Interpretation

The contracting parties may have agreed on what they said or wrote, but differed on what they meant. In fact, it is easy to realize that words are not always understood as intended and they need to be interpreted.

As a general introduction, it is worth considering that the rules about interpretation are closely connected with the conceptions of contract adopted in the various legal systems. The process of interpretation may be guided by two different approaches. In one view, precedence is given to the subjective 'will of the parties'; this is consistent with the principle of party autonomy, according to which legal obligations arise from, and are justified by, the free will of the individual. The other view gives precedence to the external fact of the words in which the will has been objectively expressed.

All modern contract law regimes shift between objective and subjective interpretation. However, the usual statement is that English law looks at the external appearance of consent (expression theory), aiming at protecting the interests of commercial convenience and security of transactions. In contrast, the civil law systems follow the will theory and so they are inclined to favour the true state of mind of the parties.

These schematic statements can be useful only as an introductory guide, because the situation is much more nuanced in the reality.

6.1 The civil law 'subjective' approach

All the civil codes dedicate specific provisions to the interpretation of contracts and they give precedence to a subjective approach. The French civil code provides that "A contract is to be interpreted according to the common

DOI: 10.4324/9781003251606-6

intention of the parties rather than stopping at the literal meaning of its words. If this intention cannot be detected, the contract is interpreted according to the meaning that a reasonable person in the same position would give to it" (Article 1188).[1] Similarly, the German BGB provides that "when a declaration of intent is interpreted, it is necessary to ascertain the true intention rather than adhering to the literal meaning of the declaration" (§ 133). The other codes reflect the same approach, sometimes giving the judge supplementary guidance. For instance, the Italian Civil Code dedicates ten articles to the interpretation of contract (1362–1371). It specifies that the contract is to be interpreted in its entirety and its terms have to be read in a harmonious way. The principle of good faith, moreover, always guides the process of interpretation. This means that when no real 'common intention' of the parties can be established the judge has the task of ascertaining what they reasonably intended, in the light of all the circumstances of the case.

Therefore, what really characterises the civil law approach is the central role of the judge, who has the task to give the 'correct' interpretation of the parties' intention. Of course, the first way to ascertain the common intention of the parties is through the letter of the contract. However, in case of uncertainty (as it very often happens), the judge's operating space is quite large. An Italian case decided by the Court of Cassation in 2018 is useful to show the wide judicial discretion.[2] In a contract of sale of a building, there was a term concerning the sale of a block of sub-plots, whereas it was clear that this was a material mistake, because the parties' intention was that their sale was only *pro quota*. After contrasting decisions from the first instance court and the court of appeal, the Court of Cassation concluded for the seller, fixing some essential rules for the interpretation of contracts:

> When the content of contract, as it is materially written, does not correspond to the common and real intention of the parties, as a result of an erroneous drafting or reporting of material facts, [...] there is a material mistake and the judge can consider all the evidence in order to reach the correct persuasion about the real and effective will of the

1 "Le contrat s'interprète d'après la commune intention des parties plutôt qu'en s'arrêtant au sens littéral de ses termes. Lorsque cette intention ne peut être décelée, le contrat s'interprète selon le sens que lui donnerait une personne raisonnable placée dans la même situation".

2 Cass. Civ., sec. II, 04/10/2018, no. 24208.

contracting parties. In these cases, the real and common will of the parties prevails over the words used.

6.2 The English 'objective' approach

The first aspect to point out while introducing the English approach to interpretation of contracts is that whereas the civil law countries' rules have a statutory nature, being fixed by the legislature through specific provisions in the respective civil codes, in the English legal tradition they are case law rules, based on precedents. The principles on interpretation are of great importance in the situation where parties have chosen to use words that have acquired an established technical meaning, but they are always to be taken cautiously and not rigidly applied.

With this caution in mind, it is relatively uncontroversial that the test adopted by English judges has an objective nature. Interpretation

> is the ascertainment of the meaning which the document would convey to a reasonable person having all the background knowledge which would reasonably have been available to the parties in the situation in which they were at the time of the contract.[3]

The intention of the parties is not determined considering their 'real' intention, but according to the contextual meaning of the relevant contractual language.

The recent UK Supreme Court judgment *Arnold v Britton*[4] is a perfect illustration of the 'objective' approach.

From 1974, the then owners of an area of land granted a number of 99-year leases of plots on which holiday chalets were to be built, the preamble to each lease stating that it would be granted "upon terms similar in all respects" to the other leases, the introductory words of clause 3 providing that each lessee's covenants as to use and repair of chalets were, inter alia, for the benefit of other lessees, and clause 4(8) containing a covenant by the lessors that the

3 *Investors Compensation Scheme Ltd v West Bromwich Building Society* [1998] 1 WLR 896, per Lord Hoffmann.

4 [2015] 2 WLR 1593. See G. Leggatt, 'Making Sense of Contracts: The Rational Choice Theory' *LQR* 2015, 454 p. 475. Emphasis is added in order to attract attention on the most relevant *dicta*.

covenants imposed on other lessees were to like effect. Clause 3 of the first group of leases included, in clause 3(2), a lessee's covenant "to pay [...] a proportionate part of the expenses and outgoings incurred by the lessors in the repair, maintenance, renewal and the provision of services [as set out in the lease] in the yearly sum of £90", increasing thereafter at a three-yearly compound rate of 10%. Subsequently, leases in respect of further chalets were granted in which clause 3(2) provided for an annual 10% compound increase. In 2011 the tenants of those chalets, whose annual service charge had risen to over £2,700 as opposed to £282 for the chalets subject to the earlier leases, and who claimed that an interpretation of the clause which required a fixed sum payment resulted in such an absurdly high annual service charge that it could not be right, claimed that clause 3(2) should be read as requiring them to pay a variable sum, being a fair proportion of the cost of providing the services, with the specified sum being no more than a cap on the maximum sum payable. The landlord commenced CPR Part 8 proceedings in the county court seeking a declaration that clause 3(2) required the payment of the fixed sum and not any lesser variable amount. The judge construed the clause in accordance with the construction contended for by the tenants and so dismissed the claim. Allowing an appeal by the landlord, the High Court judge held that, on a natural reading of the clause, the object of the verb "to pay" was the fixed sum of £90 as escalated, whereas the construction contended for by the tenants would involve rewriting the bargain which the parties had made, which, given the high levels of inflation in the United Kingdom when those leases had been granted, could not be said at that time to have lacked commercial purpose. Dismissing the tenants' appeal, the Court of Appeal affirmed the High Court judge's reasoning and held, additionally, that the words "a proportionate part" were not inconsistent with a fixed service charge in circumstances where other lessees were contributing to the overall service charge, which in consequence was to be apportioned between them.

Lord Neuberger of Abbotsbury PSC (with whom Lord Sumption and Lord Hughes JJSC agreed)

[...] 14. Over the past 45 years, the House of Lords and Supreme Court have discussed the correct approach to be adopted to the interpretation, or construction, of contracts in a number of cases starting with *Prenn v Simmonds* [1971] 1 WLR 1381 and culminating in *Rainy Sky SA v Kookmin Bank* [2011] 1 WLR 2900.

15. When interpreting a written contract, the court is concerned to identify the intention of the parties by reference to "what a reasonable person having all the background knowledge which would have been available to the parties would have understood them to be using the language in the contract to mean", to quote Lord Hoffmann in *Chartbrook Ltd v Persimmon Homes Ltd.* [2009] AC 1101, para 14. And it does so by focussing on the meaning of the relevant words, in this case clause 3(2) of each of the 25 leases, in their documentary, factual and commercial context. That meaning has to be assessed in the light of (i) the natural and ordinary meaning of the clause, (ii) any other relevant provisions of the lease, (iii) the overall purpose of the clause and the lease, (iv) the facts and circumstances known or assumed by the parties at the time that the document was executed, and (v) commercial common sense, but (vi) disregarding subjective evidence of any party's intentions. [...]

16. For present purposes, *I think it is important to emphasise seven factors.*

17. *First, the reliance placed in some cases on commercial common sense and surrounding circumstances (eg in* Chartbrook *[2009] AC 1101, paras 16–26) should not be invoked to undervalue the importance of the language of the provision which is to be construed.* The exercise of interpreting a provision involves identifying what the parties meant through the eyes of a reasonable reader, and, save perhaps in a very unusual case, that meaning is most obviously to be gleaned from the language of the provision. Unlike commercial common

sense and the surrounding circumstances, the parties have control over the language they use in a contract. And, again save perhaps in a very unusual case, the parties must have been specifically focussing on the issue covered by the provision when agreeing the wording of that provision.

18. *Secondly,* when it comes to considering the centrally relevant words to be interpreted, I accept that the less clear they are, or, to put it another way, the worse their drafting, the more ready the court can properly be to depart from their natural meaning. That is simply the obverse of the sensible proposition that the clearer the natural meaning the more difficult it is to justify departing from it. However, *that does not justify the court embarking on an exercise of searching for, let alone constructing, drafting infelicities in order to facilitate a departure from the natural meaning.* If there is a specific error in the drafting, it may often have no relevance to the issue of interpretation which the court has to resolve.

19. *The third point I should mention is that commercial common sense is not to be invoked retrospectively.* The mere fact that a contractual arrangement, if interpreted according to its natural language, has worked out badly, or even disastrously, for one of the parties is not a reason for departing from the natural language. Commercial common sense is only relevant to the extent of how matters would or could have been perceived by the parties, or by reasonable people in the position of the parties, as at the date that the contract was made. [...]

20. *Fourthly,* while commercial common sense is a very important factor to take into account when interpreting a contract, a court should be very slow to reject the natural meaning of a provision as correct simply

because it appears to be a very imprudent term for one of the parties to have agreed, even ignoring the benefit of wisdom of hindsight. *The purpose of interpretation is to identify what the parties have agreed, not what the court thinks that they should have agreed.* Experience shows that it is by no means unknown for people to enter into arrangements which are ill-advised, even ignoring the benefit of wisdom of hindsight, and it is not the function of a court when interpreting an agreement to relieve a party from the consequences of his imprudence or poor advice. Accordingly, *when interpreting a contract a judge should avoid re-writing it in an attempt to assist an unwise party or to penalise an astute party.*

21. The *fifth point* concerns the facts known to the parties. When interpreting a contractual provision, one can only take into account facts or circumstances which existed at the time that the contract was made, and which were known or reasonably available to both parties. Given that a contract is a bilateral, or synallagmatic, arrangement involving both parties, it cannot be right, when interpreting a contractual provision, to take into account a fact or circumstance known only to one of the parties.

22. *Sixthly,* in some cases, an event subsequently occurs which was plainly not intended or contemplated by the parties, judging from the language of their contract. In such a case, if it is clear what the parties would have intended, the court will give effect to that intention. An example of such a case is *Aberdeen City Council v Stewart Milne Group Ltd.* 2012 SCLR 114, where the court concluded that "any … approach" other than that which was adopted "would defeat the parties' clear objectives", but the conclusion was based on what the parties "had in mind when they entered into" the contract: see paras 21 and 22.

> 23. *Seventhly, reference was made in argument to service charge clauses being construed "restrictively".* I am unconvinced by the notion that service charge clauses are to be subject to any special rule of interpretation. Even if (which it is unnecessary to decide) a landlord may have simpler remedies than a tenant to enforce service charge provisions, that is not relevant to the issue of how one interprets the contractual machinery for assessing the tenant's contribution. The origin of the adverb was in a judgment of Rix LJ in *McHale v. Earl Cadogan* [2010] HLR 412, para 17. What he was saying, quite correctly, was that the court should not "bring within the general words of a service charge clause anything which does not clearly belong there". However, that does not help resolve the sort of issue of interpretation raised in this case".

In the light of the objective approach adopted by English courts, the possibility to make recourse to preliminary negotiations for the purposes of interpretation is also generally excluded.

To this respect, the leading English case is *Chartbrook Ltd v Persimmon Homes Ltd.*[5]

After the development was completed a dispute arose between the parties over the calculation of an "additional residential payment" ("ARP") which was defined in the contract and was payable under the terms of the contract by the defendants to the claimants. The claimants brought an action for an amount which, in their interpretation of the contract, they alleged was still owed. The judge and the majority of the Court of Appeal held that the claimants' interpretation was correct. The House of Lords allowed an appeal by the defendants and reversed the previous judgments.

The admission of pre-contractual negotiations as an aid to the construction of a contract would create uncertainty of outcome in disputes over

5 *Chartbrook Ltd v Persimmon Homes Ltd* [2009] 4 All ER 677.

interpretation and would add to the cost of advice and litigation. The law of contract was designed to enforce promises with a high degree of predictability and if conventional meanings and syntax were to be displaced by inferences drawn from pre-contractual negotiations, the less predictable the outcome was likely to be. The availability of the remedies of rectification and estoppel by convention were safeguards which would in most cases prevent any injustice caused by the exclusion of that evidence.

Lord Hoffmann

28. The rule that pre-contractual negotiations are inadmissible was clearly reaffirmed by this House in *Prenn v Simmonds* [1971] 1 WLR 1381, where Lord Wilberforce said (at p. 1384) that earlier authorities "contain little to encourage, and much to discourage, evidence of negotiation or of the parties' subjective intentions." It is clear that the rule of inadmissibility has been established for a very long time. In *Inglis v. John Buttery & Co* (1878) 3 App Cas 552, 577 Lord Blackburn said that Lord Justice Clerk Moncreiff (at (1877) 4 R 58, 64) had laid down a principle which was nearly accurate but not quite when he said that in all mercantile contracts "whether they be clear and distinct or the reverse, the Court is entitled to be placed in the position in which the parties stood before they signed". The only qualification Lord Blackburn made was to reject Lord Moncreiff's view that the Court was entitled to look at the pre-contractual negotiations because unless one did so, one could not be fully in the position in which the parties had been.
29. Instead, Lord Blackburn preferred (at p. 577) the opinion of Lord Gifford ((1877) 4 R 58, 69–70):

> Now, I think it is quite fixed – and no more wholesome or salutary rule relative to written contracts can be devised – that where parties agree to embody, and do actually embody, their contract in a formal

> written deed, then in determining what the contract really was and really meant, a Court must look to the formal deed and to that deed alone. This is only carrying out the will of the parties. The only meaning of adjusting a formal contract is, that the formal contract shall supersede all loose and preliminary negotiations – that there shall be no room for misunderstandings which may often arise, and which do constantly arise, in the course of long, and it may be desultory conversations, or in the course of correspondence or negotiations during which the parties are often widely at issue as to what they will insist on and what they will concede. The very purpose of a formal contract is to put an end to the disputes which would inevitably arise if the matter were left upon verbal negotiations or upon mixed communings partly consisting of letters and partly of conversations. The written contract is that which is to be appealed to by both parties, however different it may be from their previous demands or stipulations, whether contained in letters or in verbal conversation. There can be no doubt that this is the general rule, and I think the general rule, strictly and with peculiar appropriateness applies to the present case.

30. To allow evidence of pre-contractual negotiations to be used in aid of construction would therefore require the House to depart from a long and consistent line of authority, the binding force of which has frequently been acknowledged: see *Bank of Scotland v. Dunedin Property Investment Co Ltd* 1998 SC 657, 665 ("well-established and salutary", per Lord President Rodger; *Alexiou v. Campbell* [2007] UKPC 11 ("vouched by [...] compelling authorities", per Lord Bingham of Cornhill.) The House is nevertheless invited to

do so, on the ground that the rule is illogical and prevents a court from, as the Lord Justice Clerk in *Inglis v. John Buttery & Co* (1878) 3 App Cas 552 said, putting itself in the position of the parties and ascertaining their true intent.

31. In *Prenn v. Simmonds* [1971] 1 WLR 1381, 1384 Lord Wilberforce said by way of justification of the rule:

> The reason for not admitting evidence of these exchanges is not a technical one or even mainly one of convenience, (though the attempt to admit it did greatly prolong the case and add to its expense). It is simply that such evidence is unhelpful. By the nature of things, where negotiations are difficult, the parties' positions, with each passing letter, are changing and until the final agreement, though converging, still divergent. *It is only the final document which records a consensus*. If the previous documents use different expressions, how does construction of those expressions, itself a doubtful process, help on the construction of the contractual words? If the same expressions are used, nothing is gained by looking back: indeed, something may be lost since the relevant surrounding circumstances may be different. And at this stage there is no consensus of the parties to appeal to. It may be said that previous documents may be looked at to explain the aims of the parties. In a limited sense this is true: the commercial, or business object, of the transaction, objectively ascertained, may be a surrounding fact. Cardozo J. thought so in the *Utica Bank* case. And if it can be shown that one interpretation completely frustrates that object, to the extent of rendering the contract futile, that may be a strong argument for an alternative interpretation, if that can reasonably be found. But beyond that it may be difficult to go: it

may be a matter of degree, or of judgment, how far one interpretation, or another, gives effect to a common intention: the parties, indeed, may be pursuing that intention with differing emphasis, and hoping to achieve it to an extent which may differ, and in different ways. The words used may, and often do, represent a formula which means different things to each side, yet may be accepted because that is the only way to get 'agreement' and in the hope that disputes will not arise. The only course then can be to try to ascertain the 'natural' meaning. Far more, and indeed totally, dangerous is it to admit evidence of one party's objective – even if this is known to the other party. However strongly pursued this may be, the other party may only be willing to give it partial recognition, and in a world of give and take, men often have to be satisfied with less than they want. So, again, it would be a matter of speculation how far the common intention was that the particular objective should be realised.

33. I do however accept that it would not be inconsistent with the English objective theory of contractual interpretation to admit evidence of previous communications between the parties as part of the background which may throw light upon what they meant by the language they used. The general rule, as I said in *Bank of Credit and Commerce International SA v. Ali* [2002] 1 AC 251, 269, is that there are no conceptual limits to what can properly be regarded as background. Prima facie, therefore, the negotiations are potentially relevant background. They may be inadmissible simply because they are irrelevant to the question which the court has to decide, namely, what the parties would reasonably be taken to have meant by the language which they finally adopted to express their agreement. For the reasons

given by Lord Wilberforce, that will usually be the case. But not always. In exceptional cases, as Lord Nicholls has forcibly argued, a rule that prior negotiations are always inadmissible will prevent the court from giving effect to what a reasonable man in the position of the parties would have taken them to have meant. Of course judges may disagree over whether in a particular case such evidence is helpful or not. In *Yoshimoto v. Canterbury Golf International Ltd* [2001] 1 NZLR 523. Thomas J thought he had found gold in the negotiations but the Privy Council said it was only dirt. As I have said, there is nothing unusual or surprising about such differences of opinion. In principle, however, I would accept that previous negotiations may be relevant.

34. It therefore follows that while it is true that, as Lord Wilberforce said, inadmissibility is normally based in irrelevance, there will be cases in which it can be justified only on pragmatic grounds. I must consider these grounds, which have been explored in detail in the literature and on the whole rejected by academic writers but supported by some practitioners.

35. The first is that the admission of pre-contractual negotiations would create greater uncertainty of outcome in disputes over interpretation and add to the cost of advice, litigation or arbitration. Everyone engaged in the exercise would have to read the correspondence and statements would have to be taken from those who took part in oral negotiations. Not only would this be time-consuming and expensive but the scope for disagreement over whether the material affected the construction of the agreement (as in the *Yoshimoto* case) would be considerably increased. As against this, it is said that when a dispute over construction is litigated, evidence of the pre-contractual negotiations is almost invariably tendered in support of an alternative claim for rectification (as in *Prenn v. Simmonds* and in this case) or an argument based

on estoppel by convention or some alleged exception to the exclusionary rule. Even if such an alternative claim does not succeed, the judge will have read and possibly been influenced by the evidence. The rule therefore achieves little in saving costs and its abolition would restore some intellectual honesty to the judicial approach to interpretation.

36. There is certainly a view in the profession that the less one has to resort to any form of background in aid of interpretation, the better. The document should so far as possible speak for itself. As Popham CJ said in the *Countess of Rutland's Case* (1604) 5 Co Rep 25, 25b, 26a:

> it would be inconvenient, that matters in writing made by advice and on consideration, and which finally import the certain truth of the agreement of the parties should be controlled by averment of the parties to be proved by the uncertain testimony of slippery memory.

37. I do not think that these opinions can be dismissed as merely based upon the fallacy that words have inherent or "available" meanings, rather than being used by people to express meanings, although some of the arguments advanced in support might suggest this. It reflects what may be a sound practical intuition that the law of contract is an institution designed to enforce promises with a high degree of predictability and that the more one allows conventional meanings or syntax to be displaced by inferences drawn from background, the less predictable the outcome is likely to be. In this respect, it is interesting to consider the reaction to the statement of principle in *Investors Compensation Scheme Ltd v. West Bromwich Building Society* [1998] 1 WLR 896,912–913, which was viewed with alarm by some distinguished commercial lawyers as having greatly increased the quantity

of background material which courts or arbitrators would be invited to consider: see Lord Bingham's recent paper ("A New Thing Under the Sun: The Interpretation of Contract and the ICS Decision" (2008) 12 Edinburgh LR 374–390) and Spigelmann CJ, "From Text to Contract: Contemporary Contractual Interpretation" (2007) 81 ALJ 322. As Lord Bingham pointed out, there was little in that statement of principle which could not be found in earlier authorities. The only points it decided that might have been thought in the least controversial were, first, that it was not necessary to find an "ambiguity" before one could have any regard to background and, secondly, that the meaning which the parties would reasonably be taken to have intended could be given effect despite the fact that it was not, according to conventional usage, an "available" meaning of the words or syntax which they had actually used.

38. Like Lord Bingham, I rather doubt whether the *ICS* case produced a dramatic increase in the amount of material produced by way of background for the purposes of contractual interpretation. But pre-contractual negotiations seem to me capable of raising practical questions different from those created by other forms of background. Whereas the surrounding circumstances are, by definition, objective facts, which will usually be uncontroversial, statements in the course of pre-contractual negotiations will be drenched in subjectivity and may, if oral, be very much in dispute. It is often not easy to distinguish between those statements which (if they were made at all) merely reflect the aspirations of one or other of the parties and those which embody at least a provisional consensus which may throw light on the meaning of the contract which was eventually concluded. But the imprecision of the line between negotiation and provisional agreement is the very reason why in every case of dispute over interpretation, one or other of the parties is likely to require a court

or arbitrator to take the course of negotiations into account. Your Lordships' experience in the analogous case of resort to statements in Hansard under the rule in *Pepper v. Hart* [1993] AC 593 suggests that such evidence will be produced in any case in which there is the remotest chance that it may be accepted and that even these cases will be only the tip of a mountain of discarded but expensive investigation. *Pepper v. Hart* has also encouraged ministers and others to make statements in the hope of influencing the construction which the courts will give to a statute and it is possible that negotiating parties will be encouraged to improve the bundle of correspondence with similar statements.

39. Supporters of the admissibility of pre-contractual negotiations draw attention to the fact that Continental legal systems seem to have little difficulty in taking them into account. Both the *Unidroit Principles of International Commercial Contracts* (1994 and 2004 revision) and the *Principles of European Contract Law* (1999) provide that in ascertaining the "common intention of the parties", regard shall be had to prior negotiations: articles 4.3 and 5.102 respectively. The same is true of the United Nations Convention on Contracts for the International Sale of Goods (1980). But these instruments reflect the French philosophy of contractual interpretation, which is altogether different from that of English law. As Professor Catherine Valcke explains in an illuminating article ("On Comparing French and English Contract Law: Insights from Social Contract Theory") (16 January 2009), French law regards the intentions of the parties as a pure question of subjective fact, their *volonté psychologique,* uninfluenced by any rules of law. It follows that any evidence of what they said or did, whether to each other or to third parties, may be relevant to establishing what their intentions actually were. There is in French law a sharp distinction between the ascertainment of their intentions and

the application of legal rules which may, in the interests of fairness to other parties or otherwise, limit the extent to which those intentions are given effect. English law, on the other hand, mixes up the ascertainment of intention with the rules of law by depersonalising the contracting parties and asking, not what their intentions actually were, but what a reasonable outside observer would have taken them to be. One cannot in my opinion simply transpose rules based on one philosophy of contractual interpretation to another, or assume that the practical effect of admitting such evidence under the English system of civil procedure will be the same as that under a Continental system.

40. In his judgment in the present case, Briggs J thought that the most powerful argument against admitting evidence of pre-contractual negotiations was that it would be unfair to a third party who took an assignment of the contract or advanced money on its security. Such a person would not have been privy to the negotiations and may have taken the terms of the contract at face value. There is clearly strength in this argument, but it is fair to say that the same point can be made (and has been made, notably by Saville LJ in *National Bank of Sharjah v. Dellborg* [1997] EWCA Civ 2070, which is unreported, but the relevant passage is cited in Lord Bingham's paper in the Edinburgh Law Review) in respect of the admissibility of any form of background. The law sometimes deals with the problem by restricting the admissible background to that which would be available not merely to the contracting parties but also to others to whom the document is treated as having been addressed. Thus in *Bratton Seymour Service Co Ltd v. Oxborough* [1992] BCLC 693 the Court of Appeal decided that in construing the articles of association of the management company of a building divided into flats, background facts which would have been known to all the signatories were inadmissible

because the articles should be regarded as addressed to anyone who read the register of companies, including persons who would have known nothing of the facts in question. In *The Starsin* (*Homburg Houtimport BV v. Agrosin Private Ltd* [2004] 1 AC 715) the House of Lords construed words which identified the carrier on the front of a bill of lading without reference to what it said on the back, on the ground that the bankers to whom the bill would be tendered could not be expected to read the small print. Ordinarily, however, a contract is treated as addressed to the parties alone and an assignee must either inquire as to any relevant background or take his chance on how that might affect the meaning a court will give to the document. The law has sometimes to compromise between protecting the interests of the contracting parties and those of third parties. But an extension of the admissible background will, at any rate in theory, increase the risk that a third party will find that the contract does not mean what he thought. How often this is likely to be a practical problem is hard to say. In the present case, the construction of the agreement does not involve reliance upon any background which would not have been equally available to any prospective assignee or lender.

41. *The conclusion I would reach is that there is no clearly established case for departing from the exclusionary rule. The rule may well mean, as Lord Nicholls has argued, that parties are sometimes held bound by a contract in terms which, upon a full investigation of the course of negotiations, a reasonable observer would not have taken them to have intended. But a system which sometimes allows this to happen may be justified in the more general interest of economy and predictability in obtaining advice and adjudicating disputes* (emphasis added). It is, after all, usually possible to avoid surprises by carefully reading the documents before signing them and there are the safety nets of

rectification and estoppel by convention. Your Lordships do not have the material on which to form a view. It is possible that empirical study (for example, by the Law Commission) may show that the alleged disadvantages of admissibility are not in practice very significant or that they are outweighed by the advantages of doing more precise justice in exceptional cases or falling into line with international conventions. But the determination of where the balance of advantage lies is not in my opinion suitable for judicial decision. Your Lordships are being asked to depart from a rule which has been in existence for many years and several times affirmed by the House. There is power to do so under the *Practice Statement (Judicial Precedent)* [1966] 1 WLR 1234. But that power was intended, as Lord Reid said in *R v. National Insurance Comrs, Ex p Hudson* [1972] AC 944, 966, to be applied only in a small number of cases in which previous decisions of the House were "thought to be impeding the proper development of the law or to have led to results which were unjust or contrary to public policy". I do not think that anyone can be confident that this is true of the exclusionary rule.

43. The rule excludes evidence of what was said or done during the course of negotiating the agreement for the purpose of drawing inferences about what the contract meant. It does not exclude the use of such evidence for other purposes: for example, to establish that a fact which may be relevant as background was known to the parties, or to support a claim for rectification or estoppel. These are not exceptions to the rule. They operate outside it.

67. Since, however, I think that the judge and the majority of the Court of Appeal were wrong on the question of construction, I would allow the appeal on that ground.

6.3 The international sources approach

In the light of all of the above, we could conclude that the civil law and common law approaches are totally divergent. This would be too harsh a conclusion. Differences are not to be emphasized, because it is not uncommon that also civil law judges make recourse to more objective tests. At the same time, it would be a mistake to minimize them. That is the reason why international sources try to find a compromise, as shown by the main rules adopted by the UNIDROIT Principles and the PECL.

UNIDROIT Principles

Art. 4.1

(1) A contract shall be interpreted according to the common intention of the parties.
(2) If such an intention cannot be established, the contract shall be interpreted according to the meaning that reasonable persons of the same kind as the parties would give to it in the same circumstances.

Art. 4.2

(1) The statements and other conduct of a party shall be interpreted according to that party's intention if the other party knew or could not have been unaware of that intention.
(2) If the preceding paragraph is not applicable, such statements and other conduct shall be interpreted according to the meaning that a reasonable person of the same kind as the other party would give to it in the same circumstances.

Art. 4.3

In applying Articles 4.1 and 4.2, regard shall be had to all the circumstances, including

(a) preliminary negotiations between the parties;
(b) practices which the parties have established between themselves;
(c) the conduct of the parties subsequent to the conclusion of the contract;
(d) the nature and purpose of the contract;
(e) the meaning commonly given to terms and expressions in the trade concerned;
(f) usages.

PECL

Article 5:101: General Rules of Interpretation

(1) A contract is to be interpreted according to the common intention of the parties even if this differs from the literal meaning of the words.
(2) If it is established that one party intended the contract to have a particular meaning, and at the time of the conclusion of the contract the other party could not have been unaware of the first party's intention, the contract is to be interpreted in the way intended by the first party.
(3) If an intention cannot be established according to (1) or (2), the contract is to be interpreted according to the meaning that reasonable persons of the same kind as the parties would give to it in the same circumstances.

Art. 5:102

In interpreting the contract, regard shall be had, in particular, to:

(a) the circumstances in which it was concluded, including the preliminary negotiations;
(b) the conduct of the parties, even subsequent to the conclusion of the contract;

(c) the nature and purpose of the contract;
(d) the interpretation which has already been given to similar clauses by the parties and the practices they have established between themselves;
(e) the meaning commonly given to terms and expressions in the branch of activity concerned and the interpretation similar clauses may already have received;
(f) usages; and
(g) good faith and fair dealing.

7 Mistake

7.1 Introductory remarks

In many situations, one or both parties can incur in a mistake, affecting the subject matter of the contract, or its terms, or the identity of the other party, or the process of communication. For an example of a common mistake, imagine that the parties agree to the sale of a painting and both the seller and the purchaser think that it is by a painter of no importance, but later it turns out to be the work of a famous artist and worth x times the sale price. Is the seller able to claim back the painting? What happens if the seller failed to consult an expert? Is the legal response different if the buyer was a connoisseur? For an example of a unilateral mistake, suppose that the buyer knew, but the seller ignored, that the painting was precious. What are the consequences when the mistake is not shared by the other party?

In the various legal systems, mistake is one of the hardest topics to deal with, terminology and rules being sometimes confusing.[1]

In the civil law legal tradition, a single doctrine embraces all the categories of mistake. This is a consequence of the theoretical approach to contract illustrated in the previous chapters. In fact, according to the intention theory, contractual obligations are enforceable because the obligor intended to bind himself. Contract is the result of the parties' will and it is essential that their will is rightly formed. Mistake, fraud and violence vitiate the parties' will. As 'vices of consent', in principle they are obstacles to the formation of a contract, since they undermine a genuine intention. In practice, however, the

1 A. Burrows, *A Casebook on Contract*, 6th ed., Oxford University Press, Oxford, 2018, p. 681.

DOI: 10.4324/9781003251606-7

subjective approach is tempered by the adoption of stricter rules, especially when a mistake is not common to both parties.

In French law, despite the original formulation of the civil code, the courts soon started to grant relief only where some additional conditions, not mentioned in the code, were met. A consensus emerged to the effect that relief would be granted only where the error was excusable (the 'excusability condition') and if it was related to an aspect of the contract which the other party knew or should have known to be essential (*déterminant*) for the mistaken party (the 'awareness condition'). In time, this last condition was transformed into an even stricter one: relief would be granted only where the contract explicitly or implicitly allocated the risk of the error to the non-mistaken party (the 'implicit term condition'). With the 2016 reform, these principles are now codified. According to the new Article 1130, the vitiating elements of contract (mistake, fraud, violence) need to be essential, considering the circumstances in which the consent was given.

Italian law takes a similar approach. A mistake can vitiate the contract only if it is essential and recognizable by the other party (Art. 1428 c.c.).

Similarly, German law shows the same tension between the (assumed) subjectivist approach and the need for more objective tests. The BGB provisions governing mistake are located in Section III ('Of Juristic Acts') of the 'General Part', specifically in Title 2 on 'Declarations of Will', which precedes Title 3 on 'Contracts'. This positioning of the provisions on mistake shows that mistake affects consent and thus applies to all 'juristic acts', not just to those generating obligations (contractual or otherwise). According to § 119:

> A person who, when making a declaration of intent, was mistaken about its contents or had no intention whatsoever of making a declaration with this content, may avoid the declaration if it is to be assumed that he would not have made the declaration with knowledge of the factual position and with a sensible understanding of the case. A mistake about such characteristics of a person or a thing being customarily regarded as essential is also considered to be a mistake about the content of the declaration.

§ 120 makes clear that the same rules apply to declarations of intent that are incorrectly transmitted. These rules apply to all cases of mistake, regardless of whether the mistake was excusable or not, known or knowable to the non-mistaken party, or induced by a misrepresentation. However, rescission of contract is conditional upon compensation of the reliance interest ('Vertrauensschaden') of those who might legitimately have relied upon the declaration. In fact, § 122 establishes a form of liability without fault on the part of the mistaken party, one that is triggered solely through his claiming rescission. The obligation to compensate does not arise "if the injured person knew the reason for the voidness or the voidability or did not know it as a result of his negligence (ought to have known it)".

Moving to English law, up to the 19th century only those mistakes induced by a misrepresentation of either party, innocently or fraudulently, could vitiate consent to a contract. This principle derived from the English law's emphasis on reliance rather than consent. Since the 19th century, however, textbook writers and judges familiar with Roman and French law began to incorporate the 'alien' doctrine of mistake, making the false assumption that the English law of contract was based upon consent and agreement. The result is that now the rules sometimes appear vague and dependent upon uncertain categorizations, to the point that some authors argue that a doctrine of mistake does not exist at all.[2] This statement is perhaps too extreme, even if it is true that there is not a single doctrine applicable to all kinds of mistake, as is the case in the civil law tradition. Also in this field, it is clear that the different common law approach is focussed on the declaration theory, according to which a person who expresses himself in public must take the risk of being wrong in his appraisal of circumstances. Each party is bound by what he/she has said. Consequently, the common law approach to mistake is much narrower than the one adopted in the civil law countries, both for unilateral and common mistakes.

Rather than insisting on further details, it is useful to compare the solutions adopted by the various legal systems in some typical situations.

7.2 Misunderstandings as to the terms of the contract (the meaning of the words)

When both parties to an agreement share a fundamental error, which deprives one party (or both) of the benefits which it had tried to obtain, the

2 In this sense, see for instance C. Slade, 'The Myth of Mistake in the English Law of Contract', *Law Quarterly Review* 1954, p. 385. E. McKendrick, op. cit., p. 501 does not hesitate to state that "the law relating to the impact of mistake on the validity of a contract is a mess".

civil law systems consider that the contract is voidable. English law adopts a narrower approach. The test was restated in the Court of Appeal case *The Great Peace*[3] as follows: (i) there must be a common assumption as to the existence of a state of affairs; (ii) there must be no warranty by either party that that state of affairs exists; (iii) the non-existence of the state of affairs must not be attributable to the fault of either party; (iv) the non-existence of the state of affairs must render performance of the contract impossible; (v) the state of affairs may be the existence, or a vital attribute, of the consideration to be provided or circumstances which must subsist if performance of the contractual adventure is to be possible.

The difference between civil law and common law becomes even more significant in the case of mistake of one party, when the mistaken party did not intend to enter any transaction at all. This is a very controversial topic.

A classical hypothetical example is traditionally used in German textbooks. Assume that a person coming from another German town visits the small town Trier. While attending a wine auction, this person waves friends in the room, being not aware that according to a local custom his waving his arms indicates that he is bidding on the wine being auctioned. Consequently, he finds out that the wine in question has been 'knocked out' to him. As the mistaken party showed that he was simply waving to his friend and had no interest in the wine auction, according to the general rules it should be concluded that no contract had been entered into.

This solution, however, cannot be generalized. Let us consider, for example, a German case decided in 1984.[4] The plaintiffs were steel contractors. A bank wrote to them stating that it had undertaken to guarantee the debts of one of the firm's customers. The firm sought to enforce the guarantee, but the bank, while recognizing it had made an incorrect statement of fact, claimed that by sending the letter it merely gave a representation of factual circumstances, but it did not have any intention of being legally bound:

> in order for the obligation to provide a guarantee to be valid, it does not matter whether or not those representing the defendant [...] actually had the will to make, or were even conscious of making a declaration aimed at a legal transaction.

3 *Great Peace Shipping Ltd v Tsavliris Salvage (International) Ltd* [2003] QB 679.
4 BGH, 7 June 1984.

According to the court, the situation is to be distinguished from that occurring when a party makes a declaration without being aware that it could be understood as constituting a legal transaction, for instance, when a person gives a signal which commonly indicates purchase, but who does not even think of buying (which is precisely the situation in the 'wine auction' case examined above). In this case, the party has the choice to rescind this declaration under § 119 BGB and compensate for reliance under § 122 BGB, or to let his declaration stand and receive the counter-performance which is due. The court held that the bank could not claim that it did not intend to declare that a guarantee had been given, because a declaration can be attributed to the party who makes it only if, according to the circumstances of the case, it emerges that this party could have realised and avoided that its declaration or conduct could have been understood as a declaration of intention in good faith.

It is worth noting that according to the common law approach the solution would have been that a valid contract was formed if it could be ascertained that the auctioneer reasonably believed that it had been.

7.3 The mistaken party intended to enter a contract but stated the terms incorrectly (communication errors)

A mistake can intervene in the process of communication when one party states the terms incorrectly. In this kind of cases, all legal systems tend to admit rectification if the other party was aware. For example, if the offeror wrote 105$ but he intended 150$ and the price was discussed between the parties so that the offeree was aware that the amount was 150$, the real amount prevails in respect of the written one.

The situation is quite different if the other party was not aware. In the civil law countries this mistake can be relevant. For example, in French law if the mistaken party can show that there was no agreement on an essential element of the contract (such as price) the consequence could be to obtain from the court that the contract is declared voidable. In Italian law, this kind of mistake is treated like all mistakes: the contract is voidable if it is an 'essential' mistake and if the other party can recognize it.

On the contrary, in English law such mistakes tend to be irrelevant.

The English approach is well illustrated by the leading case *Centrovincial Estates plc v Merchant Investors Assurance Co Ltd.*[5]

Some floors of an office building were let to the Food, Drink and Tobacco Industry Training Board which had in turn underlet one floor to the defendants at a rental of £68,320 per year. The underlease contained provisions for increasing the rent after four years to the then current market value; if the parties could not reach an agreement on what this figure should be, the matter would be referred to an independent surveyor. A letter was written to the defendants stating that the 'current market rental value' of the property was £65,000 and this was agreed to constitute an offer which the defendants then went on to accept. This offer was made by the plaintiff's solicitors and was based upon a mistake, the actual price that they had meant to feature in the offer was actually £126,000. The plaintiffs then telephoned the defendants and pointed out their mistake; this was followed by a letter from the plaintiff's solicitors who pointed out that the price they had provided was an accident. The defendants, however, asserted that the contract had already been made and that they were not to know that the price offered had been a mistake. An objective approach was taken by the Court of Appeal.

Slade LJ

[...] The letter of the 22nd June 1982 constituted a formal, unequivocal and unambiguous offer made to the defendants on behalf of the plaintiffs, with an intent to create legal relations, to agree that the "current market rental value" of the demised premises [...] was £65,000 per annum. On the face of it, the letter of the 23 June 1982 constituted a formal, unequivocal and unambiguous acceptance of that offer by the defendants.

[...] It is a well-established principle of the English law of contract that an offer falls to be interpreted not subjectively by reference to what has actually passed through the mind of the offeror, but objectively, by reference to the interpretation which a reasonable man in the shoes of the offeree would place on the offer. It is an equally well-established principle that ordinarily

5 [1983] Com LR 158 (CA).

> an offer, when unequivocally accepted according to its precise terms, will give rise to a legally binding agreement as soon as acceptance is communicated to the offeror in the manner contemplated by the offer, and cannot thereafter be revoked without the consent of the other party. Accepting, as they do, that they have not yet proved that the defendants knew, or ought reasonably to have known, of their error at the relevant time, how can the plaintiffs assert that the defendants have no realistic hope of establishing an agreement of the relevant nature by virtue of the two letters of the 22 and 23 June 1982?
>
> [...] it is contrary to the well-established principles of contract law to suggest that the offeror under a bilateral contract can withdraw an unambiguous offer, after it has been accepted in the manner contemplated by the offer, merely because he has made a mistake which the offeree neither knew nor could reasonably have known at the time when he accepted it. And in this context, provided only that the offeree has given sufficient consideration for the offeror's promise it is nothing to the point that the offeree may not have changed his position beyond giving the promise requested of him.

The reasoning behind this approach is intuitive: if the law were to take into consideration whether promises were relied upon, then this would serve to deprive contractual agreements of stability until they are relied upon. This would subvert the elements of predictability, contractual stability and certainty ensured by the objective approach in its current format.

8 Breach of contract

8.1 Specific performance and/or damages

The civil law systems are familiar with a basic principle in the case of breach of contract: the performing party has the right to specific performance (or 'direct enforcement', according to another terminology often used), unless this is materially impossible (for example, if a singer refuses to sing). As far as it is possible, the law protects the interest pursued by the performing party when concluding the contract, so as to obtain performance from the other party. From this perspective, damages are considered as an unsatisfactory equivalent. If a person concludes a valid contract in order to buy a painting and subsequently the painter refuses to deliver the painting, the interest of the buyer is to have that painting, not to have the equivalent monetary compensation. That is why the legal system provides for specific performance.

In principle, the common law approach is different. Damages are the rule and specific performance the exception.[1] The reasons for such a sharp difference are closely connected with the historical evolution of contract law rules from the writ of trespass, an 'extra-contractual' remedy that was progressively extended to cover cases of breach of a contractual promise ('assumpsit'). A successful trespass action gave rise to damages. That is why, by default, damages was the relief for breach of contract. Specific performance gradually evolved only as an equitable remedy.

With these basic ideas in mind, it is now possible to distinguish between the enforcement of (a) non-monetary obligations and (b) monetary obligations.

1 J. Cartwright, *Contract Law. An Introduction to the English Law of Contract for the Civil Lawyer*, 2nd ed., Oxford University Press, Oxford, 2013, p. 265.

DOI: 10.4324/9781003251606-8

In the case of non-monetary obligations, the difference between civil law and common law described above emerges quite clearly. According to § 241 BGB, "By virtue of the obligation an obligee is entitled to claim performance from the obligor. The performance may also consist in forbearance". This rule clearly illustrates that in the case of breach the creditor has the right to specific performance, even if, of course, the option is open to a claim for damages.

A similar principle also characterizes Italian and French law. More specifically, in France the new Article 1221 of the civil code provides that

> a creditor of an obligation may, having given notice to perform, seek performance in kind unless performance is impossible or if there is a manifest disproportion between its cost to the debtor in good faith and its interest for the creditor.

This rule is interesting, because it departs from the previous approach adopted by French courts. Before the reform, French judges considered that specific performance was available even if it proved to be very expensive. Now, on the contrary, the creditor can be barred from obtaining specific performance if there is a "manifest disproportion between its cost and its interest for the creditor", provided that the debtor is in good faith.

If the obligee refuses to obey a court order to perform, some civil law systems provide with other remedies. In particular, apart from the use of force to recover a piece of movable property or to evict the defendant from an immovable one, in France the court can issue an order for a monetary penalty (*astreinte*) "to ensure compliance with its decision" (Article L 131-1 French code of civil procedure). The *astreinte* compels the debtor to pay a sum of money if he does not perform. It is usually fixed at so much per day of delay and it does not give the creditor a direct right against the debtor. In fact, the creditor has to apply to the court to obtain the money, but the money is payable to the plaintiff. This is the main difference from the German solution, where the penalty is paid into court, not to the creditor.

In contrast, as mentioned above, in English law, damages are the general remedy and specific performance is admitted only in equity and in specific cases, essentially concerning contracts for interests in land or consumer contracts.

In the case of monetary obligations, in all legal systems the sum of money which is due may be recovered, once it is due: if the plaintiff has delivered goods to the defendant or performed services for him and has not been paid the agreed price, the plaintiff may simply sue for the sum due.

Where the systems differ is over the case in which the party who is ultimately to pay indicates, before he has received the other's performance and before the price is due, that he no longer wishes to receive performance. In the continental systems the creditor usually requires the debtor to pay. In English law the situation is a bit different, because a creditor is not normally able to make an unwilling debtor perform an obligation. For example, if the parties agreed that the creditor would paint the debtor's house, but the debtor refuses admission to the house, in English law the creditor has no way of forcing the debtor to let him enter the house. Damages are the only option, but the plaintiff is expected to take reasonable steps to mitigate his loss, for instance by finding other work. However, the rule according to which the creditor has the duty not to aggrieve damages is generally accepted also in the civil law countries.

8.2 Anticipatory breach

When the parties agreed that performance should occur within a fixed time, is it possible for the performing party not to wait for the expiration of the agreed delay if it becomes evident that the other party will be unwilling to perform?

The continental civil codes did not cover this topic explicitly. The general rule followed in France and Italy precludes the possibility to terminate a contract before the expiration of the agreed delay, even if the performing party is sure that the other party will not perform. In case of an express declaration by the other party announcing non-performance, this can only enable the creditor not to give notice to the debtor (see for instance Art. 1219 Italian civil code).

However, beyond the strict rules fixed by the civil codes, the study of case law shows that judges are inclined to admit anticipatory breach. An interesting illustration of the case law approach is a case decided by the Italian Court of Cassation.[2]

A person made an irrevocable offer to buy an apartment, specifying in the details the renovation works that the seller was expected to carry out.

2 Cass., sec II, 21 December 2012 n° 23823. The translation is provided by the author.

The parties agreed for an immediate down payment and the payment of the residual price in three instalments, the last of which at the moment of the sale, to be completed by 31 December 1999. Intimated by the seller to conclude the contract of sale, the prospective buyer asked for an inspection, which revealed that the seller had not carried out the agreed work and that unexpected variations had been made. The buyer brought an action, based on various grounds, one of which was anticipatory breach of the contract. The court of first instance rejected the buyer's claim, because the definitive contract was not to be concluded until 31 December 1999, so that in March 1999 the asserted breach was not concrete . The Court of Appeal of Genova reversed this decision and the Court of Cassation dismissed the prospective seller's appeal. The appellant claimed that the Court of Appeal was wrong in considering that the prospective seller acted against good faith, arguing that as the parties fixed the date of 31 December 1999 for the delivery of the apartment, when the prospective buyer refused to conclude the definitive contract (nine months before the expiration of the agreed date) it was not possible to consider which works were incompatible with the realization of the agreed project. According to the appellant, following the reasoning of the Court of Appeal, the concept of good faith would be extended far beyond the limits of this principle, to the point to affect the builder's autonomy in the organization of his company. The Court of Cassation considered that this ground of appeal was erroneous:

A breach of contract can be actual or anticipated, indicated in English law as 'anticipatory breach', which happens before the expiry of the contractual delay for performance. Anticipatory breach depends on the violation of the duty of good faith and loyalty in the performance of contract and it consists in conduct by the debtor making the prosecution of the contractual relationship anti-economic or impossible. The Court of Appeal of Genova ascertained that the conduct of the prospective buyer was incompatible with the obligation assumed with the preliminary contract of sale, which was to sell to the other party an autonomous apartment. [...] Nor is acceptable the appellant's argument according to which the conduct in question was appreciated nine months before the delivery of the apartment, as in this period the appellant could have completed the agreed renovation works, for the reason that within the 30 March 1999 the prospective buyer had the right to detail the works that he wanted to be done.

For these reasons, the appeal was rejected with costs. In German law, anticipatory breach was introduced only with the 2002 BGB reform. § 323, sec. 4 now provides that "the obligee may revoke the contract before performance is due if it is obvious that the requirements for revocation will be met". This solution was inspired by the Convention for International Sale of Goods.[3]

In English law the doctrine of anticipatory breach is well known since the leading case *Hochster v de la Tour*.[4]

The parties agreed on 12 April 1852 to enter into the service and employ of the defendant in the capacity of a courier, on a certain day then to come, 1 June 1852, to serve the defendant in that capacity, and travel with him on the continent of Europe as a courier for three months. Before the date on which the journey was due to start, the defendant informed the plaintiff that he no longer required his services. The plaintiff sought to bring an action against the defendant for breach of contract, even if the date for performance had not been reached.

Lord Campbell C.J.

[...] the question arises, whether, if there be an agreement between A. and B., whereby B. engages to employ A. on and from a future day for a given period of time, to travel with him into a foreign country as a courier, and to start with him in that capacity on that day, A. being to receive a monthly salary

3 M. Oehm, in G. Dannemann, R. Schulze, German Civil Code (BGB), cit., § 323, no. 4, p. 533 observes that this section is copied from Art. 72 CISG.

4 [1853] E & B 678.

during the continuance of such service, B. may, before the day, refuse to perform the agreement and break and renounce it, so as to entitle A. before the day to commence an action against B. to recover damages for breach of the agreement; A. having been ready and willing to perform it, till it was broken and renounced by B. The defendant's counsel very powerfully contended that, if the plaintiff was not contented to dissolve the contract, and to abandon all remedy upon it, he was bound to remain ready and willing to perform it till the day when the actual employment as courier in the service of the defendant was to begin; and that there could be no breach of the agreement, before that day, to give a right of action. But it cannot be laid down as a universal rule that, where by agreement an act is to be done on a future day, no action can be brought for a breach of the agreement till the day for doing the act has arrived. If a man promises to marry a woman on a future day, and before that day marries another woman, he is instantly liable to an action for breach of promise of marriage; *Short v. Stone* (8 Q. B. 358). If a man contracts to execute a lease on and from a future day for a certain term, and, before that day, executes a lease to another for the same term, he may be immediately sued for breaking the contract; *Ford v. Tiley* (6 B. & C. 325). So, if a man contracts to sell and deliver specific goods on a future day, and before the day he sells and delivers them to another, he is immediately liable to an action at the suit of the person with whom he first contracted to sell and deliver them; *Bowdell v. Parsons* (10 East, 359). One reason alleged in support of such an action is, that the defendant has, before the day, rendered it impossible for him to perform the contract at the day: but this does not necessarily follow; for, prior to the day fixed for doing the act, the first wife may have died, a surrender of the lease executed might be obtained, and the defendant might have repurchased the goods so as to be in a situation to sell and deliver them to the plaintiff. Another reason may be, that, where there is a contract to do an act on a future day, there is a relation constituted between the parties in the meantime by the contract, and that they impliedly promise that in the meantime neither will do any thing to the prejudice of the other inconsistent with that relation. As an example, a man and woman engaged to marry are affianced to one another during the period between the time of the engagement and the celebration of the marriage. In this very case, of traveller and courier, from the day of the hiring till the day when the employment was to begin, they were engaged to each other; and it seems to be a breach of an implied contract if either of them renounces the engagement. This reasoning seems in accordance with the unanimous decision of the Exchequer Chamber in *Elderton v. Emmens* [4], which we have followed in subsequent cases in this Court. The declaration in the present case, in alleging a breach, states a great deal more than a passing intention on the part of the defendant which he may repent of, and could only be proved by evidence that he had utterly renounced the contract, or done some act which rendered it impossible for him to perform it. If the plaintiff has no remedy for breach of the contract unless he treats the contract as in force, and acts upon it down to the 1st June 1852, it follows that, till then, he must enter into no employment which will interfere with his promise "to start with the defendant on such travels on the day and year," and that he must then be properly equipped in all respects as a courier for a three months' tour on the continent of Europe. But it is surely much more rational, and more for the benefit of both parties, that, after the renunciation of the agreement by the defendant, the plaintiff should be at liberty to consider himself absolved from any future performance of it, retaining his right to sue for any damage he has suffered from the breach of it. Thus, instead of remaining idle and laying out money in preparations which must be useless, he is at liberty to seek service under another employer, which would go in mitigation of the damages to which he would otherwise be entitled for a breach of the contract. It seems strange that the defendant, after renouncing the contract, and absolutely declaring that he will never act under it, should be permitted to object that faith is given to his assertion, and that an opportunity is not left to him of changing his mind. If the plaintiff is barred of any remedy by entering into an engagement inconsistent with starting as a courier with the defendant on the 1st June, he is prejudiced by putting faith in the defendant's assertion: and it would be more consonant with principle, if the defendant were precluded from saying that he had not broken the contract when he declared that he entirely renounced it. Suppose that the defendant, at the time of his renunciation, had embarked on a voyage for Australia, so as to render it physically impossible for him to employ the plaintiff as a courier on the continent of Europe in the months of June, July and August 1852: according to decided cases, the action might have been brought before the 1st June; but the renunciation may have been founded on other facts, to be given in evidence, which would equally have rendered the defendant's performance of the contract impossible. The man who wrongfully renounces a contract into which he has deliberately entered cannot justly complain if he is immediately sued for a compensation in damages by the man whom he has injured: and it seems reasonable to allow an option to the injured party, either to sue immediately, or to wait till the time when the act was to be done, still holding it as prospectively binding for the exercise of this option, which may be advantageous to the innocent party, and cannot be prejudicial to the wrongdoer. An argument against the action before the 1st of June is urged from the difficulty of calculating the damages: but this argument is equally strong against an action before the 1st of September, when the three months would expire. In either case, the jury in assessing the damages would be justified in looking to all that had happened, or was likely to happen, to increase or mitigate the loss of the plaintiff down to the day of trial. We do not find any decision contrary to the view we are taking of this case. *Leigh v. Patterson* (8 Taunt. 540) only shews that, upon a sale of goods to be delivered at a certain time, if the vendor before the time gives information to the vendee that he cannot deliver them, having sold them, the vendee may calculate the damages according to the state of the market when they ought to have been delivered. If this was a sale of specific goods, the action, according to *Bowdell v. Parsons* (10 East, 359), might have been brought before that time, as soon as the vendor had sold and delivered them to another. *Phillpotts v. Evans* (5 M. & W. 475) was a similar case: and the only question there was as to the mode of calculating the damages on a breach of contract for the sale and delivery of wheat; the Court very properly holding that the plaintiff was entitled to damages according to the state of the market when the wheat was to be delivered; the Court professing to proceed upon the rule laid down in *Startup v. Cortazzi* (2 C. M. & R. 165), where no question arose as to the right to bring an action before the stipulated day of delivery on a renunciation of the contract. Parke B., whose dicta are entitled to very great weight, certainly does say in *Phillpotts v. Evans* (5 M. & W. 477), with reference to the notice by the defendants that they would not accept the corn: "I think no action would then have lain for the breach of the contract, but that the plaintiffs were bound to wait until the time arrived for delivery of the wheat, to see whether the defendant would then receive it." But the learned Judge might suppose that the notice did not amount to a renunciation of the contract; and, if he thought that, after such a renunciation, the plaintiffs were bound to proceed with the performance of the contract on their part, and to incur expense and loss in tendering the wheat before they could have any remedy on the contract, we cannot agree with him. In *Ripley v. M'Clure* (4 Exch. 345) it is said that, under a contract for the sale and delivery of goods, a refusal to receive them at any time before they ought to be delivered was not necessarily a breach of the contract: but the Court intimated no opinion upon the question whether, there being a contract to do an act at a future day, if one party before the day renounces the contract, the other thereupon has a remedy for a breach of the contract. And they held that a refusal by one party before the day when the act is to be done, if unretracted, would be evidence of a continual refusal down to, and inclusive of, the time when the act was to be done. The only other case cited in the argument which we think it necessary to notice is *Planche v. Colburn* (8 Bing. 14), which appears to be an authority for the plaintiff. There the defendants had engaged the plaintiff to write a treatise for a periodical publication. The plaintiff commenced the composition of the treatise; but, before he had completed it, and before the time when in the course of conducting the publication it would have appeared in print, the publication was abandoned. The plaintiff thereupon, without completing the treatise, brought an action for breach of contract. Objection was made that the plaintiff could not recover on the special contract for want of having completed, tendered and delivered the treatise, according to the contract. Tindal C.J. said: "The fact was, that the defendants not only suspended, but actually put an end to, 'The Juvenile Library;' they had broken their contract with the plaintiff." The declaration contained counts for work and labour: but the plaintiff appears to have retained his verdict on the count framed on the special contract, thus shewing that, in the opinion of the Court, the plaintiff might treat the renunciation of the contract by the defendants as a breach, and maintain an action for that breach, without considering that it remained in force so as to bind him to perform his part of it before bringing an action for the breach of it. If it should be held that, upon a contract to do an act on a future day, a renunciation of the contract by one party dispenses with a condition to be performed in the meantime by the other, there seems no reason for requiring that other to wait till the day arrives before seeking his remedy by action: and the only ground on which the condition can be dispensed with seems to be, that the renunciation may be treated as a breach of the contract.

Upon the whole, we think that the declaration in this case is sufficient. It gives us great satisfaction to reflect that, the question being on the record, our opinion may be reviewed in a Court of Error. In the meantime we must give judgment for the plaintiff.

8.3 Effects of termination: the problem of restitutionary claims

Concerning the effects of termination, a controversial issue is the following: when one or both parties have rendered some performance to the other before termination of the contract, will the party who has performed be able to claim restitution of what was transferred?

The different answers to this question depend on the way in which the various legal systems look at termination.

The French model (followed by the Italian civil code) considers that termination operates retroactively. Once termination is assessed, the effects of the contract are vanished and there is little difficulty in allowing restitution. The French reform of the civil code dedicates an entire section to the problem of restitution in general (Articles 1352 to 1352-9). It explicitly provides that a party who received property from the other party before the contract was terminated will have to return it or, in the case of impossibility (for instance when the property was sold), to pay its current value. The 2002 BGB reform introduced specific provisions on the effects of termination (§§ 346–348), providing explicitly that "in the case of revocation, performance received and emoluments taken are to be returned".

In contrast, English law is much less favourable to the party seeking restitution, as termination tends to be conceived prospectively only. In the case *Sumpter v Hedges*[5] a builder agreed to construct two houses for the defendant at a price of £565. He performed partially (£333 worth of this) and then he abandoned the work because of financial difficulties. The innocent party had already paid £219 and the builder claimed for payment of the rest. The Court of Appeal held that the innocent party was not obliged to pay, as his obligation only arose on completion of the work. The defendant was liable to pay for loose materials left on site, because these materials had not acceded to his land but had been knowingly appropriated by the defendant.

An attempt to change this rule by the Law Commission in 1983 was not successful, despite the dissenting opinion expressed by one of the Law Commissioners.

> Experience has shown that it is all too common for [...] builders not to complete one job [...] before moving on to the next. [Reforming the rule would] remove from the householder almost the only effective sanction he has [...]. 'Unless you come back I shan't pay you a penny'.[6]

8.4 Damages

All legal systems adopt specific rules concerning the measure of damages, together with rules giving relevance to some elements capable of reducing their amount (for instance, contributory negligence). From a comparative point of view, it is interesting to focus our attention on two issues where the rules differ substantially.

8.4.1 Notice

The first one concerns notice and it can be outlined very briefly. Civil law systems require a notice to the debtor: in principle (and besides some exceptions) the debtor will not become liable for damages until a warning has been

5 [1898] 1 QB 673.

6 Law Commission, 'Law of Contract; Pecuniary Restitution on Breach of Contract' (Law Commission No. 121, 1983).

given or a demand for performance by the creditor. This is not true for English law; as a general rule, in the case of delay, damages will run from the date on which the debtor should have performed.

8.4.2 Penalty clauses

The second issue is much more complex and it requires a more extensive account. It concerns agreed damages (penalty clauses), which are very often included as specific terms of contract.

We will start with French law. Before 1975, Article 1226 of the civil code provided as follows: "A penalty is a clause by which a person, in order to insure the performance of an agreement, promises something in case such agreement is not performed". No larger or smaller amount could be awarded to the other party. This meant that the recovery of further damages was excluded.

In 1975 a reform was introduced. It gave the judge the power both to reduce and increase the penalty fixed by the parties if it was manifestly excessive or ridiculously small (Article 1152).

After the 2016 reform, the new Article 1231-5 upholds these rules:

> Where a contract stipulates that the person who fails to perform shall pay a certain sum of money by way of damages, the other party may be awarded neither a higher nor a lower sum. Nevertheless, a court may, even of its own initiative, moderate or increase the penalty so agreed if it is manifestly excessive or derisory. Where an undertaking has been performed in part, the agreed penalty may be reduced by a court, even of its own initiative, in proportion to the advantage which partial performance has procured for the creditor, without prejudice to the application of the preceding paragraph. Any stipulation contrary to the preceding two paragraphs is deemed not written. Except where non-performance is permanent, a penalty is not incurred unless the debtor was put on notice to perform.[7]

7 "Lorsque le contrat stipule que celui qui manquera de l'exécuter paiera une certaine somme à titre de dommages et intérêts, il ne peut être alloué à l'autre partie une somme plus forte ni moindre. Néanmoins, le juge peut, même d'office, modérer ou augmenter la pénalité ainsi convenue si elle est manifestement excessive ou dérisoire. Lorsque l'engagement a été exécuté en partie, la pénalité convenue peut être diminuée par le juge, même d'office,

Similar rules are adopted in Italy. The possibility for judges to reduce *ex officio* the amount fixed by the parties is not specified in the code, but it was introduced by case law in 1995. Further damages are excluded unless expressly provided. The main difference from the French model is that the judge can only reduce the penalty, but not increase it.

German law admits penalty clauses, even if in practice German courts limit their enforceability in many ways.[8] The key rule is fixed by § 339 BGB:

> where the debtor promises the obligee, in the event that he fails to perform his obligation or fails to do so properly, payment of an amount of money as a penalty, the penalty is payable if he is in default. If the performance owed consists in forbearance, the penalty is payable on breach.

§ 340 specifies that once the obligee is entitled to damages for non-performance, the forfeited penalty is the minimum amount of damages. This means that recovery of further damages is not excluded.

In contrast with the continental approach, English law traditionally is reluctant to admit penalty clauses. A clause providing for a penalty is invalid. The creditor may then sue only for the actual loss. The only exception is if the clause was a genuine attempt to pre-estimate the loss. In this case it is valid as a "liquitated damages clause" and the creditor may recover the agreed amount even if the actual loss is less or even not existent. If the actual loss is greater than the agreed sum, the creditor cannot recover more than was agreed. Some uncertainty exists whether, if the clause is invalid as a penalty and the actual loss is greater than the penalty, the sum fixed in the penalty clause acts as a 'cap'.

The rule against penalties has recently been reshaped by a very important decision of the UK Supreme Court in *Cavendish Square Holding BV v Talal El Makdessi* and *ParkingEye Limited v Beavis*,[9] deciding two different cases.

The first case (Makdessi) involved the sale of a controlling interest in a marketing company where the defendant agreed to sell his stake to the

à proportion de l'intérêt que l'exécution partielle a procuré au créancier, sans préjudice de l'application de l'alinéa précédent. Toute stipulation contraire aux deux alinéas précédents est réputée non écrite. Sauf inexécution définitive, la pénalité n'est encourue que lorsque le débiteur est mis en demeure".

8 M. Oehm, in G. Dannemann, R. Schulze, German Civil Code (BGB), cit., § 339, p. 557.

9 [2015] 3 WLR 1373.

claimant. The defendant agreed to pay $147 million in instalments and that he would not compete with his old business and if he did, he would be owed no more instalments and the claimant would be able to purchase the remaining shares. The defendant breached the non-compete clause and the claimant sought a judgment that he was not entitled to further payments and that he should be able to purchase the shares back as agreed. The trial judge found that this term could be enforced and the Court of Appeal reversed the decision, rejecting the use of the clauses. The claimant appealed this decision on the basis that the clauses were not penal and should apply to commercial transactions, particularly where the parties had equal bargaining power.

In the second case (ParkingEye), the defendant pleaded that his vehicle was parked in a privately owned shopping centre, managed by the claimant. Notices were clearly displayed across the car park and stated that the car park was free for the first two hours but that £85 would be charged for those who wished to stay longer. The claimant brought proceedings after the defendant drove out of the car park after almost three hours and refused to pay the £85 fee as stated by the signs. The trial judge found for the claimant and the Court of Appeal rejected an appeal from the defendant which had been raised on the basis that the clause on the signs in the car park was penal and therefore was unfair. The defendant appealed again to the UKSC.

The UK Supreme Court conjoined the two cases and was required to establish the nature of the clauses in the two contracts. This required a consideration of whether the terms were penal, and therefore unenforceable, or whether the rule should be updated, abolished or restricted. It was argued by the appellants in both cases that the clauses imposed onerous restrictions on them, which was not necessarily a result of the breach of contract.

Firstly, it was held by the Supreme Court that the rule which made a penal clause unenforceable was an important and long-standing principle of English law and would therefore not be restricted or abolished in the current case. However, the Supreme Court gave a landmark judgment which amended the test to determine whether a clause was enforceable or not under the circumstances. This required assessing whether the obligations in question were primary or secondary considerations, with the innocent party being able to enforce a penal clause on the basis of a secondary obligation.

Applied to the facts, the Supreme Court found that the clauses in Makdessi were not penalties and were therefore enforceable by the claimant.

In ParkingEye, their Lordships found that the charge for overstaying was not a penalty and, again, could be enforced.

In conclusion, it is clear that significant differences emerge within the various legal systems. In essence, what should be kept in mind is that in the civil law countries penalty clauses are valid, but, at the same time, they are subject to reduction and sometimes also to increase. On the contrary, English law is diffident towards penalty clauses and behind this attitude one can see another notable consequence of the role of consideration. In fact, the key obstacle is that it is difficult for an English jurist to justify how to enforce a promise to pay an amount when this is not related to the actual damages suffered by the innocent party.

The different approaches described above produce the effect that it is difficult for the promisor to foresee the probable cost of a contemplated breach: in English law, the promisor may well hope to have the contract clause declared a penalty and thus to defeat it completely. In civil law, on the contrary, the promisor knows that at best he can obtain a reduction of the stipulated amount of penalty. Moreover, in French and Italian laws, penalty clauses limit the amount of damages (unless expressly provided), but in Germany the opposite rule applies and so, in principle, penalty clauses do not limit further damages when it is proved they have occurred. Especially in the field of international contracts, one should be aware of this important aspect. For instance, let us assume that while drafting a contract of sale between an Italian seller and a German buyer the Italian counsel considers that it is not important to specify in the contract that further damages are excluded, relying on the fact that this is the default rule according to the Italian provisions outlined above. However, if German law is applicable to the contract, in case of litigation the Italian counsel would soon discover a very different outcome because German law admits further damages by default.

9 Supervening events

9.1 Introduction

Failure to perform is not always due to the responsibility of one contracting party. It can be the result of situations where the initial conditions or events contemplated by the parties to a long-term contract subsequently change, due to a wide range of situations, whether technical, political, environmental, etc., causing the destruction of the subject matter of the contract, or its unavailability, or other problems. In these cases, the performance of contract could be radically impossible . These situations are known as 'force majeure'. Supervening events can also be due to other circumstances, not making the performance totally impossible, but much more onerous, for example because of an unforeseeable increase in costs. These kinds of situations are known as hardship or 'imprévision'.

In theory, the doctrines of force majeure and hardship are distinguishable, being based on different rationales: the former on supervening impossibility and the latter on changed circumstances rendering the performance excessively onerous. However, they are often confused. An example of this overlapping can be found in the UN Convention on Contracts for the International Sale of Goods (CISG), whose Art. 79 provides that

> A party is not liable for a failure to perform any of his obligations if he proves that the failure was due to an impediment beyond his control and that he could not reasonably be expected to have taken the impediment into account at the time of the conclusion of the contract or to have avoided or overcome it or its consequences.

DOI: 10.4324/9781003251606-9

Some scholars suggest that this provision also covers extreme cases of insurmountable economic impediments, which is a typical hardship scenario and not one of 'force majeure'. Similarly, the drafters of the UNIDROIT Principles of International Commercial Contracts (UPICC) observe that "there may be factual situations which can at the same time be considered as cases of hardship and of force majeure".[1]

We will now describe the essential rules concerning the two doctrines.

9.2 Force majeure/frustration

The original French civil code provisions did not give any definition of force majeure. Art. 1148 of the French Civil Code stated that force majeure exonerates from paying damages: "There is no occasion for any damages where a debtor was prevented from transferring or from doing that to which he was bound, or did what was forbidden to him, by reason of force majeure or of a fortuitous event". This rule was applied in a drastic way, following an 'all-or-nothing' approach: either there is a total impossibility to perform, or the debtor must perform the contract, however onerous its performance has become.

The rigorous approach adopted by French courts is well illustrated in the Court of Cassation decision, concerning a case of violent robbery that occurred in a hotel in Saint-Tropez.[2]

Four wrongdoers succeeded in gaining access to a hotel, at around 5 o' clock in the morning of 27 July 1985. They forced the staff under the threat of arms to open the safe, which they emptied. An Italian customer brought an action against the hotel and its insurer for the recovery of the equivalent of LIT 32,850,000 and US$1,030 which he said he had deposited in the hotel safe. The court of first instance rejected the claim on the grounds that armed robbery of that kind constitutes a force majeure case, but the Court of appeal reversed the first judgment and the Court of Cassation approved.

1 See the official comment under Art. 6.2.2, p. 217.

2 Cass. Civ., 1re, 9 March 1994. The original text is freely accessible through the following link: www.legifrance.gouv.fr/juri/id/JURITEXT000007031881/. The translation is provided by the author.

Whereas the company and its insurer submit that the appealed judgment was erroneous in excluding "force majeure" whilst the court ascertained that no resistance could have been offered to the armed robbery, so that it ought to have considered whether that impossibility of resistance did not of itself constitute a case of force majeure; as by holding that the hotelier ought to have carried out stricter controls of entries and exits and ought to have drawn up an inventory, in the presence of the parties concerned, of the items deposited, after finding there to have been violence and armed threats, the court of appeal, giving judgment on inoperative ground, deprives its decision of any legal basis under article 1954 of the civil code; as unforseeability is on the other hand a relative concept and not absolute in nature; as the judgment appealed against by considering that an armed robbery was not unforeseeable in a hotel in Saint-Tropez owing to its wealthy clientele, it did not attach sufficient weight to the normal unforseeability of armed aggression carried out by ruse in the hotel, and again it deprived its decision of any legal basis under the abovementioned provision;

Whereas, however, although impossibility to resist the event constitutes in itself a case of 'force majeure' where to foresee it does not enable its effects to be averted, the defendant must still have taken all the precautions necessary in order to avoid the occurrence of the event; as having found the hotelier or his agents and employees did not carry out a strict control of entries since the night watchman himself let in one of the wrongdoers who claimed to have an appointment with one of the hotel's customers, the court of appeal was right in taking the view that the armed robbery in question did not constitute a case of force majeure, since not all the possible precautions necessitated by it foreseeability had been taken.

For these reasons the Court rejects the appeal against the judgment of the cour d'appel.

After the 2016 French reform of contracts and obligations, the new Article 1218 finally defines force majeure as an event beyond the control of the debtor, preventing performance of the debtor's obligation, being unforeseeable at the time of the conclusion of the contract and whose effects could not be avoided by appropriate measures. The provision also distinguishes between temporary and permanent impossibility: in the first case, performance is only suspended, in the second case it fully discharges the parties from their obligations.[3]

German law has an even more nuanced approach. It distinguishes various categories of impossibility: initial, subsequent, objective, subjective, temporary, definitive, full and partial. A very theoretical approach leads to shaping a general doctrine on impossibility, whether or not it is attributable to the debtor. According to § 275 BGB "A claim for performance is excluded to the extent that performance is impossible for the obligor or for any other person". In contrast with the French provisions examined above, the BGB does not require the event to be unforeseeable. Moreover, German case law reveals a tendency to give more relevance to impossibility than do other legal systems.

The approach followed by German judges is well illustrated in an old decision by the Reichsgericht, 3 February 1914.[4]

The defendant sold the plaintiff 20,000 kg of sugar beet seed in June 1909, in respect of each of the following years 1910, 1911 and 1912 at the price of 26 Marks per 50 kg, to be delivered in February of each year. In February 1912 only 920 kg were delivered, because in 1911 there had been a drought and only 933.35 quintals were harvested, instead of the 4,908 expected. Since the defendant was also obliged to supply the seeds to other purchasers, he allocated the supplies on a pro rata basis to each of his customers. The plaintiff disputed the allocation thus carried out (46% of the total agreed quantity) and brought an action for performance of the contract and

3 Art. 1218: "In contractual matters, there is force majeure where an event beyond the control of the debtor, which could not reasonably have been foreseen at the time of the conclusion of the contract and whose effects could not be avoided by appropriate measures, prevents performance of his obligation by the debtor. If the prevention is temporary, performance of the obligation is suspended unless the delay which results justifies termination of the contract. If the prevention is permanent, the contract is terminated by operation of law and the parties are discharged from their obligations under the conditions provided by Articles 1351 and 1351-1 [i.e.: impossibility of performance]".

4 For this translation, © H. Beale, B. Fauvarque-Cosson, J. Rutgers, S. Vogenauer, *Cases, Materials and Text on Contract Law*, 3rd ed., London, Hart Publishing, 2019, p. 1184, an imprint of Bloomsbury Publishing plc.

the recovery of damages. The Court of first instance dismissed the plaintiff's action, the Court of Appeal set aside the judgment and upheld the claim. The Reichsgericht quashed the appealed judgment.

> It is common ground that the Summer of 1911 was marked by a drought of such extraordinary severity that harvests were very bad. Consequently, in light of the requirements of good faith laid down in § 242 and the exceptional circumstances supervening in 1911, the defendant cannot be required to do more than he can reasonably perform. Thus he was entitled to treat his customers on an equal footing and to sell his seeds on a pro rata basis in accordance with quantities ordered by each of them. It should be declared that the plaintiff's action is ill-founded and that the appeal in revision by the defendant should be granted.

The English approach to impossibility has always been very restrictive and rigorous. Prior to the mid-1800s, the rule was that subsequent impossibility is not an excuse. In 1863, in the leading case *Taylor v Caldwell*[5] the King's Bench was confronted with a performer (Taylor) who had agreed to rent a music hall for four days (owned by Caldwell). Just prior to the first concert, the music hall was accidently destroyed by fire. The court held that such an unforeseen supervening event was not caused by the fault of either party and it rendered performance impossible. The doctrine of frustration was put in the language of an "implied term" in the contract: the parties must have intended that the contract would no longer bind them if it became impossible to perform. Blackburn J developed this principle through the usual common law technique. He held that certain specific cases in which the courts had released parties from their contract because of supervening impossibility demonstrated a general underlying principle. According to Blackburn J, all contracts have a thing that is essential to them, and that thing must continue

5 [1863] 122 Eng. Rep. 309 (K.B.).

to exist throughout performance. If that thing is destroyed by no fault of the party seeking the excuse, then failure to perform can be excused.

In *Taylor v Caldwell* the frustration excuse succeeded because performance was impossible. In subsequent cases, this rule was extended also to situations where performance remained technically possible. In the well-known coronation cases, the most prominent being *Krell v Henry*,[6] the defendant agreed to rent an apartment for the purpose of viewing the coronation parade of King Edward VII, but the coronation was postponed because the King became ill; the defendant refused to pay the rent and the court held that the contract could be discharged.

The requirement of an "implied condition" was later criticized by the House of Lords, who considered that it was fictitious to say that the doctrine of frustration was based on the parties' intentions.

The modern test was set out in *Davis Contractors v Fareham*,[7] where a stricter standard was established requiring that the circumstances must "involve a fundamental or radical change" from the original contractual obligation. This strict standard still prevails today.

Requiring that the event has to render the contract "something radically different from that which was in the contemplation of the parties" is something that goes further than the idea of force majeure. In the extremely rare cases when the courts ascertain that the contract is frustrated, they adopt an all-or-nothing approach: either the contract as a whole is frustrated and the parties are released, or they remain bound and liable for non-performance.

A recent example showing this strict approach is *Canary Wharf (BP4) T1 Ltd v European Medicines Agency*.[8] It is a very long case and we will summarize it. The European Medicines Agency (an EU agency) was located in London before Brexit and then it moved to Amsterdam. It held a lease for premises in Canary Wharf, London, for a term of 25 years from August 2011. On 29 March 2017 the UK gave notice under the EU Treaty of its decision to withdraw from the EU. On 2 August 2017 the tenant wrote to the landlord stating it considered that withdrawal would be treated as an event frustrating the lease. The landlord commenced proceedings and sought a declaration that the withdrawal by the UK from the EU would not frustrate the lease. The tenant argued that the UK's withdrawal from the EU would frustrate the lease

6 [1903] 2 KB 740 (CA).
7 [1956] AC 696 [728].
8 [2019] EWHC 335 (Ch).

because: a) it would lose certain privileges and immunities under Protocol 7 and the EU Treaty; b) it could no longer lawfully be located at the premises; c) it could no longer lawfully exercise the rights conferred by the lease, including the right to assign; and d) as a result of the above, it could not meet its obligations to pay rent.

The legal basis for the tenant's argument was that the lease would be frustrated by supervening illegality or frustration of common purpose. The landlord disputed the above and argued that Brexit would not frustrate the lease. The event said to frustrate (Brexit) had not occurred at that time. Having said that, Smith J proceeded from the starting point that the UK would withdraw without further agreement from the EU on 29 March 2019. Smith J considered at length the English doctrine of frustration. In particular, he cited the general test for frustration set out by Lord Radcliffe in *Davis Contractors v Fareham Urban DC* [1956] AC 696 at 729:

> frustration occurs whenever the law recognises that without default of either party a contractual obligation has become incapable of being performed because the circumstances in which performance is called for would render it a thing radically different from that which was undertaken by the contract … it was not this that I promised to do.

And also, Lord Simon in *National Carriers Ltd v Panalpina (Northern) Ltd* [1981] 2 WLR 45:

> Frustration of a contract takes place where there supervenes an event (without default of either party and for which the contract makes no sufficient provision) which so significantly changes the nature (not merely the expense or onerousness) of the outstanding contractual rights and/or obligations from what the parties could reasonably have contemplated at the time of its execution that it would be unjust to hold them to the literal sense of its stipulations in the new circumstances: in such case, the law declares both parties to be discharged from further performance.

A significant dictum in Smith J's judgment is the following:

> Whether a contract is frustrated depends upon a consideration of the nature of the bargain of the parties when considered in the light of the

> supervening event said to frustrate that bargain. Only if the supervening event renders the performance of the bargain "radically different", when compared to the considerations in play at the conclusion of the contract, will the contract be frustrated. [...] In some cases, the supervening illegality has no effect at all on the enforcement of contractual obligations; in others, it renders the contract unenforceable by one party or the other but leaves the rest of the contract standing and enforceable; in yet others, neither party will be able to enforce the contract. In some cases, supervening illegality will cause the contract to be frustrated, but not in all.

Smith J made preliminary findings, including that the premises leased by the tenant were bespoke commercial premises. At the time of the lease negotiations, the premises had yet to be constructed and had subsequently been built to the tenant's specifications. After a thorough review of the law, including public international law, Smith J rejected the contention that the tenant would not be able to pay rent post-Brexit. In relation to supervening illegality, Smith J found that the tenant did not lack the power to continue its obligations, such as payment of rent, under the lease; even if it did lack capacity, because that related to illegality under a foreign law, namely EU law, this was not a matter that needed to be taken into consideration. The frustration is to be determined having regard to the law of the place of performance, the UK. He upheld the ratio in *London and Northern Estates Company v Schlesinger* [1916] 1 KB 20 namely that: "for supervening illegality to frustrate, it must remove all or substantially all of the benefit that one party receives from the contract".

In consideration of whether the frustration was 'self-induced' by the tenant, he found that the legal effects on the tenant of Brexit could have been ameliorated by the EU and therefore that this 'renders the frustration of the Lease self-induced'.

Then the judge came to the common purpose frustration issue. He observed that the test for common purpose frustration was that stated by Rix LJ in *Edwinton Commercial Corporation v. Tsavliris Russ (Worldwide Salvage and Towage) Ltd, The "Sea Angel"* [2007] EWCA Civ 547 at [111].

> the application of the doctrine of frustration requires a multi-factorial approach. Among the factors which have to be considered are the terms of the contract itself, its matrix or context, the parties' knowledge, expectations, assumptions and contemplations, in particular as

> to risk, as at the time of the contract, at any rate so far as these can be ascribed mutually and objectively and then the nature of the supervening event, and the parties' reasonable and objectively ascertainable calculations as to the possibilities of future performance in the new circumstances.

Therefore, Smith J stated that the question in this case was "whether there can be said to be a common purpose as between the EMA [tenant] and CW [landlord], at the time of the Agreements, going beyond what was agreed upon in the Lease, which has been rendered radically different by supervening events".

Smith J found that in this case there was no common purposes. He said:

> The Lease provided for the circumstance where the tenant may abandon its headquarters at the Premises. That outside the terms of the Lease, the parties' purposes were not common. The tenant focussed on bespoke premises, flexibility re term of the lease and lowest rent payable vs. the landlord fixed on long-term cash flow at the highest rate. Therefore, no common purpose different to that set out in the Lease.

In the field of international contracts, force majeure tends to be considered as a transnational legal principle. Not only do most international contracts contain force majeure clauses, but the force majeure doctrine is also explicitly recognized as a general principle of law by international courts (for example, the Iran-United States Claims Tribunal) and rules. As an example of this approach consider the solution adopted by the UNIDROIT Principles.

Art. 7.1.7 UNIDROIT Principles

1. Non-performance by a party is excused if that party proves that the non-performance was due to an impediment beyond its control and that it could not reasonably be expected to have taken the impediment into account at the time of the conclusion of the contract or to have avoided or overcome it or its consequences;.
2. When the impediment is only temporary, the excuse shall have effect for such period as is reasonable having regard

to the effect of the impediment on the performance of the contract.

3. The party who fails to perform must give notice to the other party of the impediment and its effect on its ability to perform. If the notice is not received by the other party within a reasonable time after the party who fails to perform knew or ought to have known of the impediment, it is liable for damages resulting from such non-receipt.
4. Nothing in this article prevents a party from exercising a right to terminate the contract or to withhold performance or request interest on money due.

9.3 Imprévision/hardship

Most legal systems provide specific mechanisms in order to deal with the change of circumstances that make the contract much more onerous. Originally, French law did not attribute any consequence to hardship ('imprévision'), nor did it allow a revision of contract by the courts.

The French restrictive approach is well described by a very famous case, known as "Canal de Craponne" (Court of Cassation, 6 March 1876).[9]

The case originates from a contract formed in 1567 between Adam de Craponne and the inhabitants of the town of Pélissanne. Mr. de Craponne constructed a canal and the inhabitants formally undertook to contribute to the costs to maintain it against a payment of three sols for every two hectares irrigated by the farmers of the town. This sum became derisory and out of all proportion to the effective costs. Mr. de Craponne's heirs sued for an increase and the lower court granted it. The inhabitants appealed and the Court of Cassation reversed the previous judgment.

9 Cass. Civ., 6 mars 1876, *De Gallifet v Commune de Pélissanne*, reported in *Les grands arrêts de la jurisprudence civile*, 12th ed., Paris, 2008, p. 183. The translation is provided by the author.

In view of art. 1134 Code civil:[10]

Whereas this article simply repeats established principles as to contractual obligations which have always been followed, its application to the present contract is not affected by the fact that it was formed prior to the promulgation of the Code; whereas the rule it enacts is general and absolute, applicable to all contracts, including those to be performed at successive periods, and that it is no part of the function of courts, however equitable it may seem to them, to modify the parties' agreements in the light of changing times and circumstances or to substitute new terms in the place of those freely accepted by the parties;

Whereas in deciding otherwise and raising to 30 centimes for the period 1834 to 1874, and from then onwards to 60 centimes the sum per unit of irrigation on the basis that the original sum of three sols fixed by the contracts of 1560 and 1567 was no longer in relation to the cost of maintaining the canal de Craponne, the decision under review has manifestly violated article 1134.

For these reasons the decision of the Court of Appeal of Aix-en-Provence is quashed.

This decision fixed a rule subsequently followed by French courts in civil cases. On the contrary, in the field of administrative contracts the administrative courts allow "révision pour imprévision" in the case of a contract whose structure is absolutely overturned owing to exceptional circumstances, provided that the event is not definitive. This means that public authorities are liable to pay compensation. The ideas behind justifying that stance are, firstly, the principle of continuity of the public service (in the absence of an adjustment the public service secured under the contract would be interrupted) and secondly the right of the person contracting with the public authorities to expect financial equilibrium within the contract.

10 Before the 2016 reform, Art. 1134 provided as follows: "Agreements lawfully entered into take the place of the law for those who have made them. They may be revoked only by mutual consent, or for causes authorized by law. They must be performed in good faith".

The 2016 reform apparently changes the *Canal de Craponne* rule. According to the new Article 1195:

> If a change of circumstances being unforeseeable at the time of the conclusion of the contract renders performance excessively onerous for a party who had not accepted the risk of such a change, that party may ask the other contracting party to renegotiate the contract. The first party must continue to perform his obligation during renegotiation. In the case of refusal or if renegotiation fails, the parties may agree to terminate the contract from the date and on the terms which they fix, or by a common agreement ask the court to set about its adaptation. In the absence of an agreement within a reasonable time, the court may, on the request of one of the parties, revise the contract or put an end to it, from a date and subject to such terms as it shall determine.

Therefore, the court is in principle allowed to modify the contract. Despite this apparent huge change, French authors stress that the reform does not innovate radically the rules concerning the change of circumstances. Moreover, since the reform has come into force, almost every contract now provides a specific term excluding the applicability of Art. 1195. Finally, the reactions to Art. 1195 forced the legislator to narrow its scope through a reform in 2018, excluding from its field of application the obligations arising from security and financial contracts.

The evolution of German law towards hardship is quite interesting. The 1900 BGB did not have any provision concerning hardship. If one party did not perform, besides in the case of impossibility, the consequence was breach of contract. However, very soon the perfect system built by the Pandectists had to cope with reality. Soon after the end of the First World War, Germany faced a big economic crisis, with an enormous devaluation of the Mark. Long-term contracts were consequently severely affected. The courts had to find a solution.

Two important cases decided after the First World War and the subsequent German economic crisis show their approach.

The first one was decided in 1922.[11] The defender M and the trader B were owners of a partnership. After dissolving the partnership, M entered

11 Reichsgericht 3 February 1922.

into relations with the plaintiff R, in order to save his investment. On 31 May 1919 a contract was entered into before a notary under which the defendant declared:

> 1. Should I acquire land and buildings having been in the ownership of the partnership on the dissolution of the partnership at a price less than or equal to RM 600.000, I shall cede to R such asset at the price at which I acquired it. 2. Should the price be higher than RM 600.000, I shall cede such asset to R for RM 600.000. In such a situation he shall pay the sum of RM 600.000 and undertakes to pay one half of the surplus to B. d. Should B acquire land and appurtenances at a price in excess of RM 600.000, I shall retain the sum of RM 600.000 payable to me, any amount over and above RM 600.000 being payable to R.

On behalf of the plaintiff, R's representative promised to pay the sale price on the transfer of the property. The contract also provided: "Should R acquire possession of the partnership, he will be in a position to employ M as a director and to guarantee him a salary to be contractually determined". R. was bound by this contract until 31 December 1919. By letter dated 12 January 1920, R's representative informed M that he regarded himself as bound by the contract beyond 31 December 1919 and that the rights under the contract continued to be in force. Through his lawyer, M stated that he was not interested. The plaintiff R brought an action, first to obtain a declaration that the contract of 31 December remained in force and that the defendant was still legally bound by it and, second, to ascertain that R's rights continued to subsist in the event that a person other than the defendant M should become the owner of the partnership. In support of this second claim, R asserted that since the partners M and B had not been able to agree on the liquidation of the partnership, the land should be sold at auction and that, moreover, the extension of the contract in such a case should be upheld.

The defendant contended that the extension of the contract should be in a notarial or judicial form and that the contract expired on 31 December 1919. The action was dismissed at first instance, but the appeal court reversed the decision and dismissed the plaintiff's claim. The problem at the origin of this case was that the amounts envisaged by the defendant became extremely high, because of the monetary depreciation which occurred since the autumn of 1919, soon after the end of the First World War. The Court explicitly referred to the doctrinal opinion expressed by Oertmann: the contract is no longer binding when the base that the parties implicitly assumed disappears.

The Reichsgericht dealt with a similar issue on 27 June 1922.[12] By notarial deed of 17 August 1894 the defendant gave a lease over land for a period expiring on 1 July 1922. With regard to stock, the contract expressly referred to the provision of §§ 587–589 BGB (according to which the stock belongs to the land and must remain there). The parties fixed at RM 113,802 the value of the whole of the stock at the end of the contract. The plaintiff brought an action to declare that the estimated value merely described the different elements and was indicative of the state of those assets; on the contrary, the stock's value had to be assessed according to their intrinsic value. The defendant claimed that the plaintiff was required to sell the stock for the agreed value, without taking into consideration the monetary depreciation.

> The collapse of the German currency is so major that [...] the gold mark which served as the basis for valuing the stock and the paper mark on the basis of which compensation is to be calculated are in no ways comparable, notwithstanding the financial parity established by the law. Neither the legal provisions nor contractual provisions enable the dispute to be resolved. The courts must be creative and deliver a judgment which accords with equity. The guiding principle must be that an equitable adjustment of the interests at stake must be made. The motives of the parties in light of the pre-war economic situation must be taken into consideration. In the present case, the extent of the stock was not in itself altered (that is to say neither increased nor diminished). Thus, the lessor may not be obliged to pay sums greater than one million RM on return of the stock solely on account of the impressive rise in prices. The value of the stock increased by only 2%. It is that added value in respect

12 Reichsgericht 27 June 1922. For this translation, © H. Beale, B. Fauvarque-Cosson, J. Rutgers, S. Vogenauer, *Cases, Materials and Text on Contract Law*, 3rd ed., London, Hart Publishing, 2019, p. 1225, an imprint of Bloomsbury Publishing plc.

of which an obligation arises for the lessor. The economic and legal principles elaborated by the RF must be observed by the courts trying the issues of fact. A decision taking into account the interests of the parties must be adopted. The case is referred back to the OLG to apply these principles of adjustment.

After German reunification, German courts were confronted with similar issues, as shown by the Bundesgerichtshof decision of 14 October 1992.[13]

The parties were former state undertakings in East Germany, which were transformed into private limited companies. Following an order by the predecessor in title of the plaintiff, confirmed by the predecessor in title of the defendant on 10 January 1990, a contract was entered into for the importation of a pressurized milling machine at an agreed price of 1,706,000 Ostmarks. Delivery of the machine was to form part of a reconstruction plan envisaged by the State. For the year 1990, the financial needs for achievement of the plan were estimated at 7,675,000 Ostmarks. 50% of the cost was to be borne by means of a subsidy and the rest by a loan. The plan (which provided for the acquisition of the machine in question) was approved by the Council of Ministers on 14 December 1989. An Austrian manufacturer supplied the machine to the plaintiff at the price of AS 2,644,259. It was then imported on 27 March 1990 and delivered to the defendant on 26 April 1990. The bank granted the defendant a loan of 1,706,000 Ostmarks. The plaintiff asked for payment of the agreed price. The defendant endeavoured to secure the financial aid provided for under the plan, but obtained only a part of the credit facility. Another bank advanced a loan of 376,809 Ostmarks, which was endorsed to the plaintiff on 29 June 1990. However, the defendant was informed that it would not be receiving any additional credit facility.

The plaintiff brought an action for payment of the agreed price, that is to say 1,706,000 – 376,809 = 1,329,191, equivalent to DM 664,597, following the monetary union on 1 June 1990. The defendant argued that it was not bound to pay, as the price was agreed before the monetary union and on

13 Bundesgerichtshof 14 October 1992. For this translation, © H. Beale, B. Fauvarque-Cosson, J. Rutgers, S. Vogenauer, *Cases, Materials and Text on Contract Law*, 3rd ed., London, Hart Publishing, 2019, p. 1228, an imprint of Bloomsbury Publishing plc.

the basis of state provisions. The Commercial Chamber of Berlin upheld the claim. On appeal, the Kammersgericht set aside the decision and ordered the defendant to pay DM 451,346 plus interest at the rate of 28%.

The BGH revised the appealed decision. It considered that the East German law could not be applied inasmuch as the law on contracts was repealed on 1 July 1990. The lower court took the view that the defendant was entitled to a reduction in price under § 242 BGB, which is applicable to contracts entered into before the entry into force of the BGB in East Germany. It was of no relevance that the defendant was unable to secure credit. Certainly, the contract provided that 50% of the acquisition would be financed by credit. However, a debtor may never plead refusal of a loan in support of financial difficulties. The decisive factor for the purposes of § 242 is that the defendant did not secure the subsidy provided for in the East German budget. At the moment when the contract was entered into, both parties had in mind that the acquisition of the machine formed part of an economic plan and that 50% would be financed by a subsidy. The contractual basis disappeared because of the failure of the plan at the time the contract was entered into and of the consequent impossibility of seeking the subsidy. With the disappearance of the subsidy corresponding to 50% of the investment, performance of the contract at the agreed price was an unforeseeable burden for the defendant. After transformation of the parties into share-capital companies, the requirements of good faith made it inappropriate to allow such a burden to be imposed on the defendant.

The BGH recalls that the contractual basis is constituted by the intentions of the two parties respectively. In this case, the intention to enter into legal relations was dependent upon the economic plan. Whilst the BGH was entitled to consider that refusal of aid did not amount to disappearance of the contractual basis, the defendant had no freedom of choice, being obliged to implement the plan. On the adjustment of the contract, the requirements of good faith have to be taken into account, in view of upholding the contract as far as possible and of adapting it to the new circumstances, in the interests of the parties.

The 2002 reform of the BGB finally codified the achievements of the German courts described so far. § 313 (Interference with the basis of the transaction) provides:

> (1) If circumstances which became the basis of a contract have significantly changed since the contract was entered into and if the parties would not have entered into the contract or would have entered into it with different contents if they had foreseen this change, adaptation

> of the contract may be demanded to the extent that, taking account of all the circumstances of the specific case, in particular the contractual or statutory distribution of risk, one of the parties cannot reasonably be expected to uphold the contract without alteration. (2) It is equivalent to a change of circumstances if material conceptions that have become the basis of the contract are found to be incorrect. (3) If adaptation of the contract is not possible or one party cannot reasonably be expected to accept it, the disadvantaged party may revoke the contract. In the case of continuing obligations, the right to terminate takes the place of the right to revoke.

The power of adaptation is the main peculiarity of the German approach. Doctrinal comments underline that the goal of adaptation must be to uphold the contract as far as possible, in order to confirm the intent of the parties when they concluded the contract. The contract will not be automatically adapted by law. The court will consider adaptation only if one party invokes its right under § 313. Therefore, it is first up to the parties to agree on which adaptation best upholds their original intention. The court will order adaptation only in case of failure of agreement.[14]

The problems experienced in Germany after the First World War suggested to the drafters of the Italian civil code in 1942 to provide for a solution. A specific article (Art. 1467) deals with supervening excessive onerous performance (*eccessiva onerosità sopravvenuta*):

> In long-term or periodic contracts, or where performance is deferred, if performance by one of the parties has become excessively onerous as a result of the occurrence of exceptional or unforeseeable events, the party whose performance is due under such terms may apply for termination of contract.

It is worth noting that in Italian law, when a court ascertains that a supervening event makes its performance too onerous, the consequence is termination of contract ('risoluzione') and no judicial power of adaptation is allowed.

Coming now to the common law approach, in principle English law holds that the parties are sovereign and that it is up to them to make their own

14 M. Oehm, in G. Dannemann, R. Schulze, German Civil Code (BGB), cit., § 313, p. 509.

provision for events that may make performance more onerous. The existence of a judicial power to adapt the contract has never been accepted. However, in specific situations the doctrine of frustration may apply. This happens only in the rare cases when the supervening events make performance of the contract impossible, illegal or radically different from what was envisaged by the parties at the time of the contract.

The English approach is very strict and the doctrine of frustration is rarely applied. The courts' reluctance is based on two reasons: a) the doctrine of frustration is "not lightly to be invoked to relieve contracting parties of the normal consequences of imprudent bargains";[15] b) contracting parties usually make provisions for the impact of unexpected circumstances and should do so themselves.

In the field of international trade, hardship is less acknowledged than the force majeure doctrine, but it is however ruled. In particular, the UNIDROIT Principles provide specific provisions regarding hardship.

Article 6.2.1 (Contract to be observed)

Where the performance of a contract becomes more onerous for one of the parties, that party is nevertheless bound to perform its obligations subject to the following provisions on hardship.

Article 6.2.2 (Definition of hardship)

There is hardship where the occurrence of events fundamentally alters the equilibrium of the contract either because the cost of a party's performance has increased or because the value of the performance a party receives has diminished, and

a) the events occur or become known to the disadvantaged party after the conclusion of the contract;
b) the events could not reasonably have been taken into account by the disadvantaged party at the time of the conclusion of the contract;

15 *Pioneer Shipping Ltd v BTP Tioxide Ltd* [1982] AC 724, per Lord Roskill.

c) the events are beyond the control of the disadvantaged party; and
d) the risk of the events was not assumed by the disadvantaged party.

Article 6.2.3 (Effects of hardship)

(1) In the case of hardship the disadvantaged party is entitled to request renegotiations. The request shall be made without undue delay and shall indicate the grounds on which it is based. (2) The request for renegotiation does not in itself entitle the disadvantaged party to withhold performance. (3) Upon failure to reach agreement within a reasonable time either party may resort to the court. (4) If the court finds hardship it may, if reasonable, a) terminate the contract at a date and on terms to be fixed, or b) adapt the contract with a view to restoring its equilibrium.

The UNIDROIT's rules show the similarity between the requirements of hardship and those of the force majeure doctrine: occurrence of an event, of whatever nature, after contract conclusion for which the obligor has not assumed the risk, unforeseeability, unavoidability and the causing by the event of an economic disequilibrium in the contract. Moreover, hardship must be "fundamental": the mere increase in cost of performance is never enough. In each individual case, according to the nature of the contract, its subject matter and the conditions of the market in which it was concluded, the judge has to determine if the event can be qualified as having caused a "fundamental" economic disequilibrium. It is worth emphasizing that the UNIDROIT Principles admit the power of adaptation of the contract by the judge, in accordance with the German rule and in sharp contrast with the common law approach.

9.4 Covid-19 pandemic: some remarks

In light of its unprecedented effects on the global economy (and, of course, the dramatic cost in terms of human lives), the recent Covid-19 pandemic is generating post-pandemic litigation and arbitration. The two classical doctrines of force majeure and hardship are called in question.

Whereas the pandemic as such is not a force majeure event, the factual or legal effects of the public health crisis may easily be qualified in terms of force majeure. The factual effects relate to illness or quarantine, death of key personnel, production facility closures, interruption of supply chains and so on. The legal effects are lockdowns, curfews, travel restrictions and other measures issued by governments and public authorities in reaction to the crisis.

The rigorous approach of French courts towards force majeure is confirmed even in the case of severe diseases as instances of force majeure. For instance, the H1N1 influenza was not considered as being unforeseeable, because it had been announced (Cour d'appel Besançon, 8 January 2014). Similarly, dengue fever has not been considered as an inevitable event, both because it is frequent and not lethal in most cases (Cour d'appel Nancy, 22 November 2010). Again, the chikungunya virus is not unforeseeable because it is easily surmountable (Cour d'appel Basse-Terre, 17 December 2018). Finally, in an Ebola case, the causal link between the pandemic and the claimed impossibility to perform has been ascertained in a very strict way (Cour d'appel Paris, 17 March 2016). Covid-19 is quite different from the examples above, and it will be possible to consider the position of the French courts only over time.

As far as English law is concerned, Covid-19 might qualify as a frustration event, in light of its global reach, systemic consequences for the global economy and resulting drastic consequences for the performance of international and domestic contracts. The pandemic and consequent governmental actions can easily fall within one or more of the cases where the courts have held contracts to be frustrated because of changes in the law (including exercise of statutory power), supervening illegality, outbreak of war, cancellation of an expected event and abnormal delay outside what the parties could have reasonably contemplated at the time of contracting. For example, where time is essential to the correct performance of the contract, the temporary unavailability of stocks or staff may arguably give rise to a frustrating event. Similarly, the performance of certain obligations could be illegal due to governmental restrictions, and this may potentially give rise to a claim of supervening illegality.

It is more difficult to envisage hardship/imprévision. In order to succeed in the case of litigation, it will be necessary to claim and demonstrate that due to the pandemic and the consequent restrictions, a fundamental economic imbalance occurred, rendering the non-performance excusable.

10 The Vienna Convention for International Sales of Goods (CISG)

10.1 Introduction

Sale of goods is perhaps the most widespread contract in cross-border transactions. Therefore, the different contract law regimes outlined in the previous chapters can hamper the development of international trade. For this reason, many initiatives have been made in order to achieve a harmonization.

Soon after the Second World War, two Conventions were prepared and adopted at The Hague in 1951, but they were not successful, as only few countries ratified them. The United Nations Commission on International Trade Law (UNCITRAL) decided to launch an entirely new project, which led to the adoption of the United Nations Convention on Contracts for the International Sale of Goods, during a conference held in Vienna in 1980. This Convention is now in force in 96 countries and it is perhaps the most well-known and widespread international legislation in the field of private law.[1] This wide consensus is the first reason for dedicating the last part of this book to a short analysis of its main contents.

The CISG was not ratified by the United Kingdom, notwithstanding many common law countries have adopted it (United States, Australia, Canada, etc.). This is a second reason why it is worth considering it. Its study is a good exercise for appreciating the weight of the different approaches to contract law examined in the previous chapters and to realize how they can be overcome. In fact, the Convention solutions are often the result of the efforts made in order to reach a compromise between the common law and the

1 The status of ratifications is constantly updated. For details see https://uncitral.un.org/en/texts/salegoods/conventions/sale_of_goods/cisg/status. Last accessed 5 November 2021.

DOI: 10.4324/9781003251606-10

civil law solutions.[2] The aim of this Chapter is not to give a comprehensive overview, but simply to introduce to the most relevant issues.

The two goals inspiring the Vienna Convention are to ensure legal certainty and to promote international trade. As explained by UNCITRAL, small and medium-sized companies located in developing countries often do not have access to a lawyer when negotiating a contract. These companies may also be the weaker contractual party. The CISG aims at levelling the playing field in contractual law by creating a fair and uniform regime.

The Convention is divided into four parts: Part I (Articles 1–13) introduces the scope of application and general provisions, Part II (Articles 14–24) describes the formation of contract, Part III (Articles 25–88) describes more detailed rules for issues that often arise in contracting and Part IV (Articles 89–101) contains the final provisions.

The CISG is not a private international law text, setting uniform rules in order to determine which law and which jurisdiction will be applicable to the contract. Rather, it is a substantive law convention. It sets forth binding substantive rules, to be applied in one and the same manner to trans-border situations, having connections with more than one country. Consequently, in every legal system having adopted the Convention, the rules concerning the contract of sale of goods are to be distinguished in two categories: domestic rules are applicable to national contracts, whereas the CISG applies to international sales of goods falling within its field of application. This has important consequences. For example, the Italian Court of Cassation recently stated:

> In cases concerning international sales of goods, reference is to be made to the Vienna Convention (CISG), as it contains material uniform rules, applicable regardless of the domestic international private law rules [...]. It follows that if the contract refers to the application of German law, this does not mean that the Convention is not applicable, because CISG is an integral part of German law.[3]

2 Some authors suggest that the CISG is a model for future attempts of harmonization. In this perspective, A. Chianale, 'The CISG as a Model Law: A Comparative Law Approach', *Singapore Journal of Legal Studies* 2016, p. 29.

3 Cass., sec. II, 25 January 2018, no. 1867.

10.2 Interpretation and scope of application

The Convention dedicates specific rules to its interpretation. This is a very important aspect to highlight. Everyone experiences that judges often interpret the same national statutory provisions in different ways. At an international level, this problem is even more accentuated, because inevitably judges tend to interpret texts according to the concepts which are familiar to their own legal system. The outcome can be that the same article is applied differently according to the national judge who interprets it. Therefore, it is essential to promote a uniform interpretation, thus limiting the risk that the process of interpretation of the CISG leads to diverging rules.

The Convention significantly promotes an autonomous style of interpretation in its Preamble:

> the adoption of uniform rules which govern contracts for the international sale of goods and take into account the different social, economic and legal systems would contribute to the removal of legal barriers in international trade and promote the development of international trade.

Article 7 then prescribes as follows:

> In the interpretation of this Convention, regard is to be had to its international character and to the need to promote uniformity in its application and the observance of good faith in international trade. Questions concerning matters governed by this Convention which are not expressly settled in it are to be settled in conformity with the general principles on which it is based or, in the absence of such principles, in conformity with the law applicable by virtue of the rules of private international law.

The duty to achieve a uniform application implies that national judges should be familiar with the case law of the other Contracting States. To this end, it is essential to provide for simple and accessible tools of research. One of them is the UNIDROIT Institute database *Unilex*, which classifies many cases from various Contracting States and provides their translation in English. The cases reported in this chapter are all taken from this very useful database.[4]

Moving now to the scope of application of the Convention, Article 6 makes clear that the parties may "exclude the application of this Convention or [...] derogate from or vary the effect of any of its provisions". However, unless the parties expressly waive or opt out of its application, the CISG applies to the contract for the sale of international goods if the parties are from different States that have ratified the CISG or the parties included the CISG in the choice of law clause of the contract. Moreover, the failure to negotiate out or to select the CISG as a choice of law in the contract may have unfavourable consequences for one or both of the parties.

One should not take for granted when a sale of goods is 'international'. The internationality of a contract depends on the relevant criteria set forth by the applicable rules. Article 1 provides that the Convention is applicable when the parties have their place of business in different Contracting States. It follows from this rule that the Convention is not applicable when the parties have their relevant places of business in the same state, even if the performance of the contract involves different states. On the other hand, it can be applicable even in cases where the goods do not cross any border and/or the parties have the same citizenship.

The notion of 'place of business' is central to ascertaining whether the Convention is applicable. Notwithstanding it is not explicitly defined, the 'place of business' is the place where there is the stable business organization, where commercial activities are carried out, characterized by a certain duration, stability and autonomy. In this sense, a liaison office is not a 'place of business', because it does not have the autonomy required. As specified in Article 10, the relevant place of business is the one having the closest relationship with the contract. Moreover, according to Article 1, the internationality of the contract must be apparent to both parties.

Beside its direct application, according to Article 1(1)(b), the Convention is also indirectly applicable if the forum's conflict of rules result in the application of the law of a Contracting State. Article 95 allows states to declare that, in this event, they do not want to be bound. A few states declared this reservation (among them, the United States of America).

4 The website is freely accessible: www.unilex.info/.

The Convention is also applicable if the parties explicitly agree that they want their contract to be ruled by it. Finally, in the absence of a choice of law clause, arbitral procedural rules may allow the tribunal to deem that the CISG applies as the appropriate law or as evidence of international usages.

An Italian case is illustrative of what has been described above.[5]

A Chinese buyer bought industrial equipment from an Italian seller. The buyer paid the price in advance, but the seller failed to deliver the goods within the period contractually agreed upon. The buyer then sued the seller claiming for termination of contract, restitution of the purchase price plus damages. After confirming its jurisdiction over the case, the Court addressed the issue regarding the applicable law. In so doing, the Court noted that the buyer, in its pleadings, had relied on Italian domestic law provisions, as Italian law was the controlling law according to the relevant conflict-of-law rules. However, in the case at hand the requirements were satisfied by the application of the CISG. In fact, both parties had their place of business in Contracting States (Art. 1(1)(a) CISG); and also the substantive requirements for the application of the Convention were met, i.e. that the contract was a contract for the sale of goods and the parties had not excluded its application, either expressly or impliedly. Such requirements being satisfied, the CISG had to be considered, by its nature, as taking precedence over uniform rules of private international law. As to the merits, the Court found it proved that the seller had failed to deliver the goods within the period agreed upon or, in any case, within a reasonable time after the conclusion of the contract. First, the seller had not contested the buyer's argument that delivery had to be effected within two weeks from payment, as also evidenced by a document issued by the buyer before contract conclusion. Secondly, even considering that the parties had not reached an

5 Tribunale of Forlì, 12 November 2012, www.unilex.info/.

agreement on the time of delivery, the result would not change. In fact, documents and declarations exchanged between the parties before contract conclusion, like the one issued by the buyer in the case at hand, must be used as an aid in interpreting the "reasonable time" within which delivery has to be effected according to Art. 33 CISG, all the more so when – as in the case at hand – the seller was aware, or could not have been unaware, that time of delivery was of essence for the buyer. The Court further held that, as a consequence of the seller's failure to deliver the goods, the buyer was entitled to terminate the contract (Art. 25 CISG), and to recover damages according to Arts. 74 & 75 CISG. For every single issue addressed by it, the Court relied on a number of decisions on CISG already rendered by foreign courts and arbitral tribunals.

In the absence of an express definition of sale of goods by the Convention, it can be implicitly defined as the contract pursuant to which one party (the seller) is bound to deliver the goods and transfer the property in the goods, and the other party (the buyer) is obliged to pay the price and accept the goods. Various Convention provisions clarify the notion of sale of goods. Within its field of application are contracts for the delivery of goods by instalments, but not distribution agreements. The term 'goods' clearly excludes immovable property, but also intangible goods (industrial property rights, a membership interest in a limited liability company), as explicitly stated by Article 2d. For example, hardware is certainly included, but one may question software, which tends to be included in the field of application of the Convention if it is made available by means of tangible support.

A very interesting topic is whether mixed contracts are covered or not by the Convention. There are borderline situations where it is difficult to distinguish if the contract in question is to be considered a sale of goods or not. For example, in Italian law when goods are to be manufactured for the client's needs, the contract can be not qualified as a sale of goods, but as a different type of contract (*appalto*) consequently applying different rules. Article 3 states as follows:

> Contracts for the supply of goods to be manufactured or produced are to be considered sales unless the party who orders the goods undertakes to supply a substantial part of the materials necessary for such manufacture or production. This Convention does not apply to contracts in which the preponderant part of the obligations of the party who furnishes the goods consists in the supply of labour or other services.

What emerges from this rule is that a contract may fall within the Convention's field of application even if this would not be the case if the contract was to be qualified according to Italian law.

Article 2 specifies that the Convention:

> does not apply to sales:(a) of goods bought for personal, family or household use, unless the seller, at any time before or at the conclusion of the contract, neither knew or ought to have known that the goods were bought for any such use; (b) by auction; (c) on execution or otherwise by authority of law; (d) of stocks, shares, investment securities, negotiable instruments or money; (e) of ships, vessels, hovercraft or aircraft; (f) of electricity.

A last preliminary aspect to consider concerns the scope of the Convention. According to Article 4, it only governs the formation of the contract of sale and the rights and obligations of the seller and the buyer arising from such a contract, but it is not concerned either with the validity of the contract and with the transfer of property in the goods sold. One should not be surprised by such a provision, because the topic of transfer of property is one where the differences between the various systems are more sensible. The option adopted by the drafters of the Convention was simply to circumvent this aspect and to concentrate their attention on the transfer of the risk of perishment of the goods sold.

10.3 The formation of contract

The Convention dedicates the entire Part II (Art. 14–24) to the formation of contract. Article 14 introduces the requirements of offer and acceptance for the formation of a contract. A "proposal for concluding a contract" constitutes an offer if: 1) it is addressed to at least one specific person; 2) the offeror has indicated an intention to be bound in the event of acceptance; and 3) the offer is sufficiently definite because it indicates the goods and expressly or implicitly makes provisions for determining quantity and price. If the offer addresses an indefinite group of people, then Article 14 requires "a clear indication of whether it is an offer". Otherwise, it is treated as merely an invitation to make an offer. With respect to the sufficient definiteness requirement, Article 14 allows the offeror to "implicitly fix or make provisions for determining the price". An offeror's communication may be an offer even if it refers to the price as being listed in a catalogue if there had been a prior course of dealings or the usage of trade recognizes the price as being set out in the catalogue.

Under Article 14, also a subjective element is required for the formation of contract. It requires some manifestation of the readiness of the offeror to be bound in the case of acceptance. Article 8 explains how this intent can be shown: statements made by and other conduct of a party are to be interpreted according to the understanding that a reasonable person of the same kind as the other party would have had in the same circumstances. In determining the intent of a party or the understanding a reasonable person would have had, due consideration is to be given to all relevant circumstances of the case including the negotiations, any practices which the parties have established between themselves, usages and any subsequent conduct of the parties. The offeror's intent to be bound can be demonstrated recurring to all the relevant extrinsic evidence outside the document, even taking into account the statements and the conduct of the parties both during negotiations as well as after the contract. In addition, the parties' intent to be bound can also be shown by usages and practices that the parties have established between themselves or that are regularly observed in their particular industry. However, in circumstances where there are no indications of the parties' intent, the court or arbitrator should "apply the objective criterion of an understanding that a reasonable person would attribute to the statements and conduct of the party, i.e. to the contract, in the equivalent circumstances".

Under Article 15 of the CISG, "[a]n offer becomes effective when it reaches the offeree". The offer is generally revocable, but the revocation has to allow a reasonable person to understand it. Moreover, the revocation must reach the addressee before the acceptance (hence, if the contract is already concluded, no revocation is possible (Art. 16.2). In the case of irrevocable offer (e.g. words like 'fix' or 'irrevocable'), the revocation will be ineffective.

To constitute an acceptance, the offeree's statement or conduct should indicate assent to the offer. Under Article 18 of the CISG, an offeree's acceptance is "[a] statement made by or other conduct of the offeree indicating assent to an offer". Therefore, absolute silence or the offeree's failure to follow up on an earlier expression of interest does not count as acceptance.

An acceptance becomes effective at "the moment the indication of assent reaches the offeror … within the time [the offeror] has fixed or, if no time is fixed, within a reasonable time" and thus concludes the offer. The purpose of this requirement is to ensure that the offeror has the opportunity to learn of the offeree's acceptance of his offer.

An offeree's acceptance is not subject to any form requirements and may be proven by any means. Under Article 11 of the CISG, oral agreements not evidenced in writing for the sale of goods are still enforceable: "A contract of sale need not be concluded in or evidenced in writing and is not subject to any other requirement as to form. It may be proved by any means, including witnesses". Therefore, the ascertainment on the formation of contracts is to be decided on the basis of the substance of the agreement rather than of its form.

Due to the lack of form requirements, a contract may be concluded or evidenced by electronic communications. The wording of Article 13 reflects the situation at the time of its drafting (in the 1980s), when the main forms of electronic communications were telegram and telex. However, the broad definition of 'writing' under Article 13 certainly includes e-mails and other modern electronic communications.

Under Article 18 the acceptance can be both through statement and by conduct. Silence does not amount to acceptance. Examples of conduct amounting to acceptance are the dispatch of an invoice, the signature thereof by the buyer, the cashing of a cheque sent with the offer, the processing of the goods by the buyer, etc.

Concerning the moment of conclusion of the contract, the CISG accepts the receipt theory (Art. 23).[6]

10.4 The obligation to deliver conforming goods

In Part III, the Convention provides for interesting rules concerning the duty to deliver conforming goods and the duty to examine them by the buyer. The relevant articles are the following.

6 See Chapter 4, §4.2.

Article 35

(1) The seller must deliver goods which are of the quantity, quality and description required by the contract and which are contained or packaged in the manner required by the contract.

(2) Except where the parties have agreed otherwise, the goods do not conform with the contract unless they:

   (a) are fit for the purposes for which goods of the same description would ordinarily be used;

   (b) are fit for any particular purpose expressly or impliedly made known to the seller at the time of the conclusion of the contract, except where the circumstances show that the buyer did not rely, or that it was unreasonable for him to rely, on the seller's skill and judgement;

   (c) possess the qualities of goods which the seller has held out to the buyer as a sample or model;

   (d) are contained or packaged in the manner usual for such goods or, where there is no such manner, in a manner adequate to preserve and protect the goods.

(3) The seller is not liable under subparagraphs (a) to (d) of the preceding paragraph for any lack of conformity of the goods if, at the time of the conclusion of the contract, the buyer knew or could not have been unaware of such lack of conformity.

Article 38

(1) The buyer must examine the goods, or cause them to be examined, within as short a period as is practicable in the circumstances.

(2) If the contract involves carriage of the goods, examination may be deferred until after the goods have arrived at their destination.

(3) If the goods are redirected in transit or redispatched by the buyer without a reasonable opportunity for examination by him and at the time of the conclusion of the contract the seller knew or ought to have known of the possibility of such redirection or redispatch, examination may be deferred until after the goods have arrived at the new destination.

Article 39

(1) The buyer loses the right to rely on a lack of conformity of the goods if he does not give notice to the seller specifying the nature of the lack of conformity within a reasonable time after he has discovered it or ought to have discovered it.

(2) In any event, the buyer loses the right to rely on a lack of conformity of the goods if he does not give the seller notice thereof at the latest within a period of two years from the date on which the goods were actually handed over to the buyer, unless this time limit is inconsistent with a contractual period of guarantee.

These articles raise many issues, as the Convention largely uses vague terms ("fit for the purpose", "reasonable time", and so on), open to diverging interpretations. Some cases will be useful for illustrating their concrete application.

The first case comes from France.[7] A French importer bought fibre-cement plates from an Italian manufacturer. These plates were resold on to another French company and used in the manufacture of coverage for two agricultural plants. A dispute arose between the parties as the goods turned out to be defective. The CISG was applicable under Article 1(1)(a).

7 Cour d'appel de Rennes 2 February 2018 (www.unilex.info/case.cfm?id=2171).

The Court found that the buyer had lost its right to rely on the lack of conformity, since it had failed to give notice thereof within the two-year time limit provided for by Art. 39(2) CISG. In reaching such a conclusion, the Court recalled that the cut-off period in Art. 39 of the Convention does not constitute a limitation period, rather only a time limit within which defectiveness must be notified. Also, the Court noted that the mere fact that the seller was the manufacturer of the goods was not sufficient to give rise to a presumption that it knew the defects and had concealed them to the buyer (Art. 40). Indeed, that provision refers to the bad faith or gross negligence of the seller, which is up to the buyer to demonstrate. Finally, the Court rejected the buyer's contention that the period indicated in Art. 39 CISG, which starts to run from the day of delivery, infringes against the rule of fair trial as established by Art. 6 of the European Convention on Human Rights (ECHR). In the Court's view, in fact, the possible neutralization of the effects of Art. 39 by virtue of Art. 40, together with the possibility opened to the parties to derogate from, or vary, the effects of the CISG's provisions in accordance with Art. 6, safeguard the interests of the buyer and ensure reasonable proportionality between the means employed and the intended purpose, compatible with the system of the ECHR.

Another interesting case was decided by an Italian court.[8] An Italian buyer bought food products from a Chilean seller. A dispute arose between the parties, as the goods on their arrival at the buyer's premises turned out to be damaged. The Italian court declared that the dispute was to be settled in accordance with the CISG's provisions, as Chile and Italy were both Contracting Parties to the Convention (Art. 1(1)(a)).

8 Tribunale di Trento 29 May 2015 (www.unilex.info/case.cfm?id=2139).

The Court rejected the seller's argument that the buyer had failed to notify the lack of conformity of the goods within a reasonable time as required by Art. 39 CISG. In this respect, the Court observed that, in order for the buyer to meet the requirements set forth by Art. 39 CISG, it was sufficient that it had informed the seller by telephone of the defects immediately after it had received the goods at its premises. The contention that a written notification of the alleged defectiveness was sent only two months after the products' delivery was therefore considered ungrounded.

Similarly, a Spanish case[9] addresses an international contract between an Italian seller and a Spanish buyer for the sale of a machine forming part of a production line making air conditioning ducts. The parties were in dispute concerning the machine's lack of conformity: once installed, it had failed to produce a single part.

With regard to the application of the Convention, the court considered that the Convention on the law applicable to contractual obligations (the Rome Convention) was subordinate to special regulations such as CISG, a special, uniform substantive law on the international sale of goods, of which both Spain and Italy—the countries where the parties were based—were contracting States (CISG art. 1 (1)(a)). Moreover, the contract in question related to the international sale of goods in the terms set out in CISG article 3 (1): the machine was manufactured in Italy, dismantled for transportation and reassembled in Spain. The fact that the goods to be delivered were prefabricated or preproduced did not change the fact that the contract in question was a sales contract and, if the buyer did not provide the

9 Fuenlabrada Court of First Instance 2012 (www.unilex.info/case.cfm?id=1824).

materials, that also constituted strong grounds for calling the contract a contract for the sale of goods (Judgement of the European Court of Justice, 25 February 2010).

The judge also referred in general terms to the interpretative tools of CISG, making it clear that domestic law was not applicable in matters governed by the Convention and could not even be cited for interpretative purposes, since that would run counter to the principle of uniformity of application (CISG art. 7 (1)). He also emphasized that legal practitioners were helped in their work of interpretation by the United Nations Commission on International Trade Law (UNCITRAL), with its Case Law on UNCITRAL Texts (CLOUT), and the digest of case law on the United Nations Convention on the International Sale of Goods (2012) was a particularly useful reference tool. He further stated that the case law of any country that could be invoked but was not grounded in the Convention would have doctrinal value but could not add anything to the Convention.

After considering the evidence, and particularly the expert reports submitted by the parties, the judge held that it was a matter of common sense that the component parts of an air conditioning duct should be assembled with sufficient precision to prevent the escape of the air circulating through it, regardless of whether or not there were rules governing the margin of tolerance for this kind of part. If the machine was not fit for the purpose for which it had been bought owing to the malfunctioning of the roller system, it must be considered a breach by the seller. It may be noted that the judge also gave due consideration to the fact that machine design was not in the buyer's line of business; the buyer did not have any qualified staff, nor had it provided proper training for operators, nor any manuals, nor had it participated in designing of the machine, although it had informed the seller of the use to which it proposed to put it. For all these reasons, the judge considered that there had been a breach of CISG article 35 (2).

The judge dismissed the seller's claim that CISG article 9 (2) applied with regards to presumptive evidence. The court flatly dismissed this claim, since CISG article 9 (2) had nothing to do with presumptive evidence and, in any case, the applicable article would be CISG article 35 (3), inasmuch as the seller knew of the defect or could not have been unaware of it. It also held that the buyer had complied with the provisions of CISG article 39, in that it had not been possible to find the defect until the machine was in operation, so the defect had remained hidden.

Furthermore, it held that the date from which the time limit was calculated (dies a quo), as laid down in article 39 (2), had not even started, since there had been no formal recognition of the buyer's taking possession of the machine and its accessories, in the form of documentation relating to occupational safety protection. The judge also considered that, in the case of non-perishable goods, or where a delay did not adversely affect the seller's activities vis-à-vis third parties, the dies a quo of the "reasonable time" referred to in article 39 was the moment at which the buyer became certain, rather than merely suspecting, that the machine did not work (here he cited Saarbrücken Regional Court, 1 June 2004, and Forli District Court, 16 February 2009). Moreover, the dies a quo should be different in the case of goods requiring a period of training and regular repairs (here he referred to the District Court for the Southern District of Ohio, United States of America, 26 March 2009, and Versailles Court of Appeal, 29 January 1998).

With regard to the claim by the seller that there had been a double or reciprocal breach on the part of the parties, in that the seller had not paid the full amount, the judge said that, in such cases, it was necessary to determine which breach was the more serious, in order to reach a decision or dismiss a claim. The court applied the criteria laid down in the doctrine on the matter—chronology, causation and proportionality—and ruled that the breach on the part of the seller was the more serious and that the buyer's was caused by the seller's. The judge considered that the seller's breach was fundamental (CISG art. 25), so the action for avoidance (CISG arts. 45 (1)(a) and 49 (1)(a)), which was taken within a reasonable time (CISG arts. 26 and 49 (2) (b)), was appropriate and was supported by CISG case law.

As for the effects of the avoidance, the judge considered the various sections of CISG article 81. With regard to the question of damages, the court considered the various claims, in the light of CISG articles 74–77 and in some cases accepted them and in others dismissed them outright for lack of evidence.

With regard to interest, the court took the majority position, on the basis of CISG article 78 and the digest of case law on the Convention, that the issue was outside the scope of the Convention and that there appeared to be a clear trend to apply the rate that would be applicable according to the rules of private international law if the Convention were not applicable. In the current case, that would mean the rate under Italian law.

Finally, a Dutch case is interesting, because it involves an English company (it is to be remembered that the UK never ratified the Convention).[10] A Dutch company (seller) and an English company specialized in the cultivation of fruit (buyer) signed a contract for the sale of 500,000 strawberry plants. After the goods had been delivered, the buyer refused to pay the outstanding price alleging that the goods had suffered water mould (a very contagious plant disease) and therefore could not grow as they were expected to. The seller challenged that the defectiveness of the plants was imputable to the buyer. As the parties had agreed on the application of the Convention, the Court confirmed that the CISG was the governing law pursuant to its Article 1(1)(b).

With respect to the seller's argument that its standard terms had been incorporated into the contract, the Court found that the buyer had had a reasonable opportunity to take notice of them.

10 Rechtbank Oost-Brabant 28 February 2018 (www.unilex.info/case.cfm?id=2162.

Even though such terms were written in Dutch, the fact that the company director was Dutch had made possible for it to read and understand such terms before signing the confirmation order to which they had been attached. In reaching such a conclusion, the Court referred to the CISG-AC Opinion no. 13 (Inclusion of Standard Terms under the CISG).

The Court then addressed the issue as to whether the buyer had fulfilled its obligation of notifying lack of conformity according to Art. 39 CISG. After pointing that Art. 39 CISG requires notice being specific as to the nature of the alleged defects, the Court denied that the buyer's notification satisfied such a requirement. In fact, whereas during the legal proceedings the buyer indicated water mould as the cause for non-conformity, it was written in the notification sent to the seller that the plants had been damaged by reason of cold storage. Nor had the buyer informed the seller of the water mould within a reasonable time from it had discovered it. As a result, the Court found that the buyer had not acted in compliance with Art. 39 CISG.

10.5 The notion of 'fundamental breach'

In case of breach, two options are conceivable in the different models of contract law, related to the standard of performance that the obligor in a sales contract has to abide by in order to discharge himself.[11] In most legal systems, the traditional rule is to require perfect tender. The disadvantage of this rule is that the creditor may opportunistically take advantage of the difficulties encountered by the other party. For this reason, the Convention adopts another rule: there is no breach if the creditor is satisfied by substantial performance.

More specifically, the CISG distinguishes (implicitly) between the consequences deriving from a simple non-fundamental breach and the remedies available only in the event of a fundamental breach. In both cases, when one

11 See Chapter 8.

party has not fully performed, the breach is ascertained through a regime of strict liability.

Article 25

A breach of contract committed by one of the parties is fundamental if it results in such detriment to the other party as substantially to deprive him of what he is entitled to expect under the contract, unless the party in breach did not foresee and a reasonable person of the same kind in the same circumstances would not have foreseen such a result.

A Polish case well illustrates the various issues in case of breach.[12]

The parties entered into negotiations for the conclusion of two contracts for the sale of cod fish (contracts N. 505 and 506). During negotiations, the Polish seller requested that an outstanding debt in the amount of €8,842.35, owed by a German subsidiary of the UK buyer, would be satisfied by the latter before the delivery of cod under the new contracts would take place. It was, however, unclear whether this request effectively became a contractual obligation. The UK buyer made a bank transfer of €8,842.35; nevertheless it expressly stated that the transfer was a prepayment for contracts N. 505 and 506. The buyer also sent the seller a document in which it was provided that 50% of the price of the goods would be paid upfront and the other half would be paid 15 days after delivery. The seller signed and returned the contracts N. 505 and 506, with an amendment according to which the specification of goods should be provided the following day. The buyer did not react to this amendment, but correspondence on packaging and labelling was exchanged between the parties. A few days later, however, the seller informed the buyer that it would not perform the contracts because no prepayment had been made and no specification of goods provided. The buyer sued for damages resulting from the seller's failure to deliver. The District Court found that no contracts were concluded and dismissed the claim. The Court of Appeals disagreed and found that under the principle of freedom of form (Article 11 CISG) there is no reason to treat the contracts as inexistent. The Court found,

12 Supreme Court of Poland 28 November 2013 (www.unilex.info/case.cfm?id=1993).

however, that the seller was entitled to avoid the contracts and dismissed the buyer's claims. The buyer appealed to the Supreme Court that considered two issues: the deadline to make a prepayment of 50% of the price in light of the standards of interpretation set forth in Article 8 CISG, and whether the seller was entitled to avoid the contract under Articles 25 and 64(1)(a) CISG.

With respect to the first issue, the Supreme Court noted that there are two standards of interpretation under Article 8 CISG and that priority should be given to the subjective standard, i.e. statements must be interpreted according to the intent of the party making the statement, if the other party knew or could not have been unaware what that intent was. Only if it is not possible to establish the meaning of such statement, the objective standard comes into play, so that statements are to be interpreted according to the understanding that a reasonable person of the same kind as the other party would have had in the same circumstances.

In the case at hand, the parties had not expressly provided in the contract the deadline for making the agreed prepayment of 50 per cent of the price. It was thus arguable whether the prepayment should have been made at the time the goods were made ready for shipping or before that time. The Court examined the correspondence between the parties and did not find anything to support the view that the parties intended to set the day when the goods were to be shipped as the date of prepayment. Rather, it resulted that the prepayment was to be made "in advance", i.e. before the goods were made ready for shipping. The Court also noted that in commercial transactions, "prepayment" normally means payment of part of the price before the goods are dispatched to the buyer. However, regardless of this last finding, the Court stated that it was the subjective standard of interpretation that prevailed in this case, since the seller clearly meant that half of the price is paid before the goods are made ready for the shipping (and the buyer was aware of the intent).

The second issue related to the fundamental breach of contract as a prerequisite for avoidance. The Supreme Court extensively discussed the nature of fundamental breach under Article 25 CISG stressing that in order to justify avoidance, the breach must relate to a contractual obligation. Therefore, since the lower courts did not establish whether the request to make a payment of €8,842.35 to satisfy the third party's debt constituted a contractual obligation of the buyer, it was impossible to verify whether in the case at hand the failure to make such a payment could be classified as a fundamental breach of contract.

The Court further stated that the notion of a fundamental breach should be interpreted restrictively in order to preserve the existence of the contract. The parties must act in good faith and cannot take advantage of the other party's failure of performance in order to terminate the contract, unless as a result of such failure, the party not in breach would be deprived of the possibility to achieve the economic aim of the contract. The breach of an obligation which can be remedied by the aggrieved party cannot, thus, be treated as fundamental. In the case at hand, the failure of the buyer to provide specification of the goods could not be treated as a fundamental breach of contract, because the seller could make the specification itself, in accordance with Article 65 CISG. Only if that was impossible, the seller could rely on Articles 25 and 64(1)(a) CISG and avoid the contract.

The Supreme Court also held that failure of payment of the goods does not usually constitute a fundamental breach. Only if the failure cannot be remedied, it can be treated as such. Therefore, failure of making a prepayment, if the buyer has not irrevocably declared that it refuses to pay, cannot be classified as a fundamental breach.

For these reasons, the judgment of the Court of Appeals was reversed and the case was remanded for further consideration.

The Convention does not define 'simple breach'. The difference between simple and fundamental breach is that only the former entitles the aggrieved party to avoidance of the contract (Art. 49 and Art. 64).

Both for fundamental and simple breaches, the available remedy is claim for performance (Art. 46 and Art. 62). The CISG adopts the civil law approach, in that it makes the claim for performance generally available. Anyway, Article 28 provides for a compromise solution:

> If, in accordance with the provisions of this Convention, one party is entitled to require performance of any obligation by the other party, a court is not bound to enter a judgement for specific performance unless the court would do so under its own law in respect of similar contracts of sale not governed by this Convention.

If the seller delivers the very quantity of goods agreed upon, but their quality does not meet the contractual specifications, a request must be filed in a reasonable time. The reasonableness of a claim for repair is to be ascertained having regard to all the circumstances of the case (for instance: the costs of reparation compared to other remedies, such as price reduction or damages).

Another remedy is price reduction, which is a self-defence. Article 50 provides the following: "If the goods do not conform with the contract and whether or not the price has already been paid, the buyer may reduce the price" in the same proportion as the value that the goods actually delivered had at the time of the delivery bears to the value that conforming goods would have had at that time. However, if the seller remedies any failure to perform his obligations in accordance with article 37 or article 48 or if the buyer refuses to accept performance by the seller in accordance with those articles, the buyer may not reduce the price.

Suspension of performance is another self-defence remedy (Art. 71–72)

10.6 Damages

Article 45 grants to the buyer the right to claim damages and Article 61.1.b grants the same right to the seller. The claim for damages can concur with any other remedy.

The principle that inspires the Convention is full compensation. Damages recoverable are both the reduction in the assets that existed at the time of the conclusion of the contract (expenditures such as costs for handling and storing non-conforming goods, banking fees for retransfer of payments, costs for repair) and the increase in assets that performance of the contract would have made possible but that the breach prevented. The courts are called upon to make a hypothetical comparison between the situation resulting from the breach and what the same situation would have been in the event that the contract had not been breached. The recoverable losses are only those that are a 'consequence' of the breach and foreseeable.

The parties are free to derogate to these rules, for example through exemption clauses and limitations of liability or penalties and liquidated damages clauses. These clauses are not governed by the Convention, so their validity depends on the domestic law identified by virtue of the conflict-of-law rules of the forum.

Article 79 deals with exemptions from liability.

(1) A party is not liable for a failure to perform any of his obligations if he proves that the failure was due to an impediment beyond his control and that he could not reasonably be expected to have taken the impediment into account at the time of the conclusion of the contract or to have avoided or overcome it, or its consequences.

(2) If the party's failure is due to the failure by a third person whom he has engaged to perform the whole or a part of the contract, that party is exempt from liability only if:
    (a) he is exempt under the preceding paragraph; and
    (b) the person whom he has so engaged would be so exempt if the provisions of that paragraph were applied to him.

(3) The exemption provided by this article has effect for the period during which the impediment exists.

(4) The party who fails to perform must give notice to the other party of the impediment and its effect on his ability to perform. If the notice is not received by the other party within a reasonable time after the party who fails to perform knew or ought to have known of the impediment, he is liable for damages resulting from such non-receipt.

The question arises if economic hardship is relevant. The CISG does not equate the term 'impediment' only with an event that makes performance absolutely impossible. However, price fluctuations are a normal risk. The consequence is that the obligor who failed to perform is not liable for damages. The other party may exercise any other available remedy.

A German case is interesting for illustrating the above rules.[13]

A German seller and an Italian buyer, both professional car dealers, entered into a contract for the sale of a used car. The seller had purchased the car from another car dealer and had submitted the vehicle registration document to the police for a preliminary check. Although nothing was revealed by the police check, it later turned out that the car had been stolen prior to its sale. As a result, the Italian police returned the car to its original owner. In the meantime, the buyer, having resold the car to a third party, had to give back the two cheques received as payment for the car. The buyer then filed a suit claiming breach of contract plus damages and lost profits. The seller requested the dismissal of the claim, alleging that it had acted in good faith.

The Court of first instance dismissed the claim, holding that, according to Art. 79(1) CISG (which, pursuant to its Art. 1(1)(a), was the law applicable to the merits of the dispute), the seller was not liable. In fact, the seller demonstrated that its breach of contract was due to an impediment beyond its control which could not reasonably be expected to have been taken into account at the time of the conclusion of the contract or avoided or could its consequences be overcome. The buyer appealed.

The Court of appeal partially reversed the decision of the Court of First Instance, finding that the seller had failed to perform its obligation, namely the transfer of ownership of the car to the buyer. After pointing out that CISG does not govern the effects of the contract on the property in the goods sold (Art. 4(b) CISG) and that, as a consequence, this is a matter governed by domestic law, the Court applied German law, which prohibits the acquisition of stolen property, even by those who pay value and are in good faith. Contrary to what the Court of First Instance affirmed, the Court of Appeal held that the seller could not be exempted from liability under Art. 79 CISG, since such an exemption implies the occurrence of objective circumstances

13 Oberlandesgericht München 5 March 2008 (www.unilex.info/case.cfm?id=1342).

preventing the fulfilment of the contractual obligations, while in the case at hand the alleged circumstances were of a subjective nature. Moreover, the argument that the alleged impediment could not reasonably be expected to have been taken into account at the time of the conclusion of the contract was not convincing. In fact, the low price of the car, the mileage and the disparities in the owner's name (which was different from the one on the registration document) should have led the seller to doubt about the ownership of the vehicle.

Accordingly, the buyer was held entitled to damages under Arts. 45(1)(b) and 74 CISG, including loss of profit.

Another interesting case comes from Spain.[14] A Spanish seller and a Belgian buyer entered into a long-lasting commercial relationship regarding the supply of pine kernels. In 2012, the seller claimed that it was able to supply only a part of the quantity agreed upon due to a conifer blight that had reduced the harvest and increased prices, as well as to problems encountered with some partners. As a result, a dispute arose between the parties.

The Court of First Instance found for the seller, which based its defence on Art. 79 CISG. The buyer appealed.

The Appellate Court overturned the first instance decision. In so doing, it rejected the seller's argument that its failure to perform was excused under Art. 79 CISG. In the Court's view, indeed, the problems the seller had encountered with the members of cooperatives did not fall within the scope of Art. 79 CISG, as such a circumstance remained within the seller's control, as it related to its organization and system of production.

Considering the high volatility in the pine kernel market, the Court also reached the conclusion that a reduction in production

14 Audencia Provincial de Valladolid 6 April 2015 (www.unilex.info/case.cfm?id=1951).

was not an event that could not be expected or avoided and that, for this reason, the seller might have protected itself from that risk by introducing into the contract terms as to delivery and price reflecting the pine kernel market features.

Furthermore, the Court concluded that the seller had been in a position to fulfil its obligations under the contract, because it had declared itself willing to deliver the missing quantity of the goods if the seller had consented to a price adjustment. Nor could the seller succeed in claiming that its failure to perform was due to the buyer's refusal to renegotiate the price, as this latter was under no obligation to accept a price other than that contractually stipulated.

A final remark. The CISG does not distinguish between principal and ancillary obligations. Even the violation of an obligation which is not a principal obligation, but an ancillary one, can be fundamental (for instance: breach of an exclusivity agreement clause, or agreed re-import prohibition). The general principle is that avoidance of the contract in cases of fundamental breach should constitute an *ultima ratio* remedy.

Index

Made in the USA
Monee, IL
18 October 2026

66036443R10118